The Bermuda Railway

Gone – But Not Forgotten!

by

Colin A. Pomeroy

Front Cover: The remains of Frank's Bay Trestle - October 1992.

Frontispiece: Front Street, Hamilton - The winter of 1938-1939.

By the same author:

"Isle of Wight Railways - a *Then & Now* Photographic Survey"
Silver Link Publishing, 1991. (ISBN 0-947971-62-9)

"British Railways Past and Present Special - Isle of Wight"
Silver Link Publishing, 1993 (ISBN 1-85895-004)

Copyright: Colin A. Pomeroy

ISBN 0 9521298 0 9

Published by Colin A. Pomeroy.

First published in June 1993.

For Bill and Rosa,

For whom I have the greatest admiration.

Best Regards Carl.

Rosa Hoth 1993

MAP OF THE BERMUDA RAILWAY

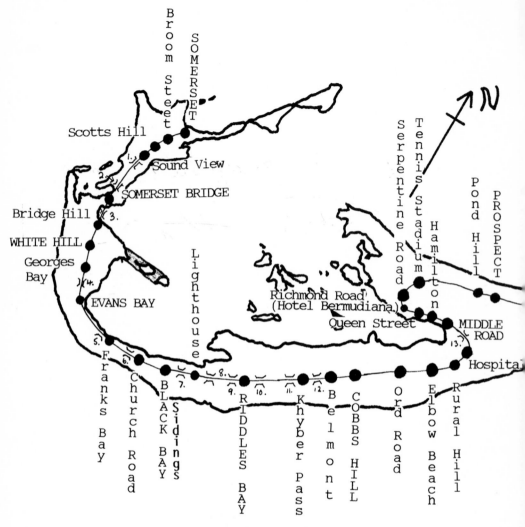

Bridges & Trestles (West)

1: Harman's Bay Trestle
2: Parapet Trestle
3: Somerset Bridge
4: Evan's Pond Trestle
5: Frank's Bay Trestle
6: Church Road Trestle
7: Mallory Trestle
8: Lighthouse Trestle
9: Riddle's Bay Trestle
10: Sharp's Trestle
11: Warwick Pond Trestle
12: Morgan's Trestle
13: Springfield Trestle

Notes:

1. Numbers refer to Bridges and Trestles.
2. Passing Loops at stations shown in capital letters.

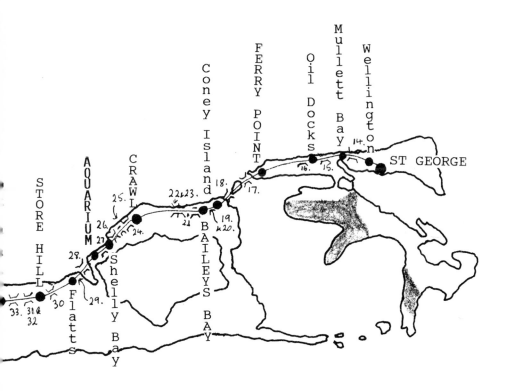

Bridges & Trestles (East)

14: Mullet Bay Trestle
15: Gulley Trestle
16: Oil Docks Trestle
17: Ferry Point Bridge
18: Coney Island Bridge
19: Henry's Hill Bridge
20: Outerbridge's Trestle
21: Bailey's Bay Trestle
22: Clay's Bay Trestle
23: Sisson's Trestle
24: The Crawl Trestle
25: Burchall Cove Bridge
26: Five Mile Trestle
27: Shelly Bay Trestle
28: Flatts Bridge
29: Flatts West Trestle
30: Store Hill Trestle
31: Gibbons' Trestle
32: Cox's Trestle
33: Devonshire Trestle

I N D E X

(Photographic acknowledgements appear on Page 117)

INTRODUCTION

It was when, as a very young member of a Royal Air Force Shackleton aircraft crew, that I first landed at Kindley Field in 1963 and heard tales of a railway having once existed in Bermuda. My first impression was that the line must have been a narrow gauge one! Recurring visits over the years have allowed me to build up a picture of the trains that once graced this beautiful mid-Atlantic chain of islands and now, as the 50th anniversary of the closure of the line rapidly approaches, it seems to me appropriate to try and bring the railway back to life - if only via the printed word and photograph.

I hope that this book will encourage those who are too young to remember much of Bermuda's old railway system to seek out the links with the past that still exist and, equally, I hope that the book will bring back fond memories for those who are lucky enough to remember the Bermuda Railway before its final demise in 1948. Finally, of course, I hope that the book will prove interesting to the thousands of tourists who visit Bermuda, allowing them an insight into what ran along *The Railway Trail* before the mopeds and joggers!

I have tried to relate between British and North American terminolgy whenever possible to avoid confusion; however, the following may be of some value:

British Terminology	American Terminology
Sleeper(s)	*Tie(s)*
Points	*Switches*
Shunting	*Switching*
Passenger Coach	*Passenger Car or Trailer*
Freight Wagon	*Box Car*
"Large Open Wagon"	*Gondola*
Guard/Ticket Collector	*Conductor*

Clyffe,
Dorset,
England.

June 1993.

A C K N O W L E D G E M E N T S

So many people, at home in the UK, in Bermuda, in Guyana, the USA, and Canada have given me cheerful help, encouragement and advice that it would be wrong for me to draw attention to any one individual; nevertheless, I must make particular reference to Bill Kitchen, Rosa Hollis (to both of whom I have dedicated my book), C Spanton Ashdown and Ray Corley, for without their assistance the book would be much less comprehensive than it is.

I also offer, in alphabetical order, my very sincere thanks to the following who have, by their kindnesses, made this book possible: Horst Augustinovic, Annette Biermann, Peggy Cheval, John Cox, John Crofts Snr, John Cross, Nick & Jenny Dicks, Anthony Eastwood, Michael Forand, Bill Hackney, Karla Hayward, Richard Hercamp, Brendan Hollis, Tony Humphreys, Peter James, Michael Jourdain, Flo Lins, James McKey, Alan Merrells, Bill & Eileen Meshau, Patty Pearce, Leon Pearman, Ron Redman, Sandra Roujas, Albert Peachey, Sandra Seenan, Dora Simpson, Arthur Swainson, John Thomas, Keith Turner, Brian Waite, David Whatley, Karen Williams, and Glen & Judy Williams. To anyone whom I have omitted above, my apologies are extended as well as my thanks.

Finally, I must thank my wife "Binks" who, once again, has allowed me to wander off and do my own thing!

H I S T O R Y   O F   T H E   L I N E

BACKGROUND - THE EARLY DAYS

Although the first recorded suggestion of a railway to serve the islands of Bermuda was made in 1893 by an American living in St George by the name of Mark Golinsky, and a formal scheme for a railway was discussed by the Public Works Department as early as in 1899 - both in the heady Victorian days of *Railway Mania* - it was only with the increase in tourism and of general economic activity after the 1914-1918 Great War that the matter was given really serious consideration. Bermuda's transportation problem was a peculiar one, for in 1908 The Motor Car Act had banned all but a very few official vehicles from the island's roads - yet dollar-earning tourism was on the increase and the ability for tourists and residents alike to move freely about Bermuda by public transport became a very obvious requirement.

Before the finally agreed upon railway system was initiated other ideas were considered, including an extensive omnibus network and a major extension to the system of local ferries. These were turned down on the grounds of local acceptability and of practicality: it was feared that noisy buses would frighten the horses in widespread use in both urban and rural areas, and that even the most efficient of ferry services could only serve locations with suitable landing sites - which still left the passengers with the problem of moving inland from the coast to their final destinations.

It was in 1910 that Canadian entrepreneurs formally proposed the formation of The Bermuda Trolley Company to operate an electrified tramway system joining together both ends of the islands, but their scheme failed to get off the ground - as had another by The Bermuda Electric Light, Power & Traction Co Ltd. This left the way open for the Government to engage William Foxlee, a British surveyor and engineer, to produce a consultation document entitled "A Report on a Bermuda Light Railway", in which he assessed the various options open to the Colony for a mass transport system (as it would be called today). He weighed the merits of road transportation against those of a railway and came down firmly in favour of the latter, partly influenced, of course, by the restrictions of The Motor Car Act.

Foxlee proposed a narrow gauge (3'6") system, which would run from Somerset to Hamilton, roughly along the line of the present Middle Road, and then drop down to follow the South Shore Road as far as Watch Hill Road (just to the east of Spittal Pond) before running alongside Harrington Sound to Flatts. After crossing Flatts Inlet, Foxlee's route to St George would have followed that which was finally chosen for the project, meeting with a 3 mile loop from the area of Watch Hill Road, via Tucker's Town and the eastern side of Harrington Sound, in the region of Bailey's Bay - and Foxlee's motive power would have come from steam tank engines!

Finally though, on 4th August 1924, the Bermuda Legislature granted permission to The Bermuda Railway Company (the "statuatory" company) for the building of a standard gauge (4'8½") railway from Somerset to St George, via Hamilton, but without the Tucker's Town loop - the franchise period being one of forty years. The all-embracing and monopolistic nature of the proposed franchise brought much strong protest from members of the Bermuda House of Assembly, with numerous attempts to scupper the plans on the grounds of legal and procedural technicalities, but the bill was eventually passed and the way lay ahead for the railway to be constructed.

The Railway Company was granted powers to aquire the necessary land for the trackbed, but landowners were loathe to let their ground go at anything less than "mark up" prices, which ultimately led to much of the track being laid on trestles and bridges at the foreshore edge in order to stay within budget. Despite such problems, construction work on the line commenced in 1926, but by early 1927 it was obvious that the original 1928 target date would not be met and the Company asked for an extension until 22nd June 1929, together with even more powerful franchise powers - which again raised a chorus of protests. The timbers for the construction of the wooden trestles, meanwhile, had arrived in Bermuda aboard the *SS West Cape*.

The shares prospectus of Bermuda Traction Ltd of 26th

June 1928 makes interesting reading. Originally seeking £125,000 Ordinary £1 Shares and £380,000 worth of Debenture Stock (£430,000 authorised), all but a handful of investors in the line came from outside Bermuda. Perhaps the locals were too shrewd to buy and could foresee the financial problems that were to lie ahead?

Even at this early juncture, the future financial viability of the undertaking was being questioned, and in 1930 the Acting Governor said in a letter to the Colonial Office in London "As regards the merit of the undertaking......, even in favourable conditions, it will be most unlikely that the railway could yield a return on anything like the whole of the capital now sunk into it".

On 19th December 1927 The Bermuda Railway Act, 1927 was passed, extending the time for construction and opening to the public until the requested June 1929 date, in return for the depositing of bonds to the value of £20,000 in London within six months - this money to be forfeited if the new target date was not met. At the same time, this new act granted the Company powers to operate mechanically-powered road vehicles for public use if the Motor Car Act was repealed and imposed upon it the responsibility of building and operating an extension of the line to the Naval Dockyard if required so to do by the military authorities.

CONSTRUCTION AND LAYOUT

As work on the line slowly proceeded - with time targets regularly failing to be met - it became necessary once more to seek approval for the opening target date to be set back yet again, finally to as late as 20th January 1932, (although the Legislature did not enforce the forfeiture of the deposited bonds). Continually, arguments ensued as to the value of land and rights of way being aquired - using up valuable construction time and draining away the Company's financial resources.

By May of 1930 only 3 miles of track had been fully completed and 50% of the track bed graded to final standards - although most of the bridge and trestle construction had been completed and all the rails and sleepers for the remaining 19 miles of track had been laid out ready for use. Estimating that 55% of the work prior to acceptance had still to be carried out, the world famous Balfour, Beatty & Company, of London, took over the construction of the line and with their expertise moved things ahead more rapidly towards completion. Their initial assessment of the quality of the work already carried out on the permanent way was not, to say the least, encouraging. The originally-laid rails were rolled in 1915 to meet low Russian standards of construction, had already seen use and had been exposed to the elements for some 15 years or so; additionally, some even inferior sections of rail had been aquired from doubtful sources! The sleepers (ties) had been laid untreated, and were much too far apart to afford the rails proper support, and little attempt had been made to ballast effectively or to provide adequate drainage. Furthermore, many of the cuttings were poorly constructed and in many places the minimum right-of-way widths had not been adhered to. (So poor was the line in fact, that a programme of major rail and sleeper replacement was initiated in 1932, whilst effective ballasting was only carried out during the course of routine track maintenance after running commenced).

The line laid was of 67½lb per yard metals, flat bottomed and spiked (as opposed to screwed) to wooden

Prior to the opening of the line to Somerset, a construction train proceeds slowly across the Springfield Trestle. Note the passengers!

sleepers, with very little level or straight running. Gradients were as severe as 1:50 in some places; there were numerous curves, of varying radii, but smoothness of ride was sought by extensive spiralling at these points. Partially due to the problems of land aquisition and partially by design, the line crossed inlets and bays at 11 different places - necessitating an inordinately large number of bridges and trestles for so few track miles: over 10% of the line was carried above ground or water on a series of 33 trestles and bridges - of which 12 were of wholly timber construction and the remaining 21 of metal, or metal and wood, design. In addition to the 1,004 foot Ferry Point Bridge, with its swing span allowing passage of boats from the Great Sound into Ferry Reach and Castle Harbour, other massive structures included the Springfield Trestle, the high Somerset and Flatts Bridges (both 40' above mean sea level to allow for the passage below of sailing vessels) and the lengthy bridge at Coney Island.

The 40'high Somerset Bridge, with the Great Sound beyond, viewed from the world famous (highway) Somerset Bridge - the smallest drawbridge in the world.

At ground level the line crossed the public highway at 30 different points, all to be unmanned, whilst open subways carried the line below general ground level twice between Serpetine Road and Tennis Stadium Stations. A short, but tightly curving, tunnel carried the track below the south west corner of Par-La-Ville Gardens, but the main tunnel was a 450 foot "cut and cover" construction at Rural Hill. This was originally planned to just be a cutting but, after a wall collapsed in 1930, it was covered over.

The whole of the 21.76 miles of railway were single track, with a series of 14 passing loops, fitted with spring operated entrance switches, allowing for the crossing of trains between the terminii. Control of access to the 15 block sections was by a Tyler & Co key token system, each section being controlled by a pair of key token instruments of the "trainman operated" variety and complemented by an Erickson magneto-ringer, battery operated, telephone system to Train Control. The sole authority for a train to proceed into a block section was possession of the key token, and the ability of the trainman to extract the key from the instrument was dependent on the condition of the pair of interlocking instruments, ie: if the other key was or was not already extracted. A safety device in the key token instruments made simultaneous extraction at both ends impossible. The instruments were provided with three position electrical indicators, which showed the state of traffic movements in the block in question.

Bermuda rolling stock under construction at the Dick Kerr Works, Preston in 1929.

An additional intermediate key token instrument was provided in the control cabin of the swing bridge at Ferry Point, on the Bailey's Bay Station to Ferry Point Station block, to protect against the bridge being

opened whilst a train was in section or for a train to
enter the section when the bridge was open to shipping.

Prior to shipment to Bermuda, one of the two "Series 60" (later
"Series 100") motor locomotives stands,with two "toast rack" passenger
trailers at English Electric's Dick Kerr works, Preston, Lancashire.

Forty-one scheduled, public passenger stops were
provided for (see Appendix B), together with a private
halt to serve Government House and a number of
privilege halts (so called because these stopping
places had been provided in some manner of exchange for
running rights over private land). Of the station
buildings, at least 10 were not completed on schedule
but were erected or completed after the line was opened
to the public.

The railway workshops were located at East Broadway, on
Middle Road between Hamilton and the Springfield
Trestle. The main building was steel framed, with
asbestos cement panels, and covered two tracks, one of
which straddled a small maintenance pit - above which
was provided a manually operated 10 ton crane, which
was fitted with an electric hoist and pull chain
control in 1933. Three storage roads were also
provided, as well as a random collection of utility
buildings: offices, stores and workshops.

A sketch map of the yard is at Appendix E.

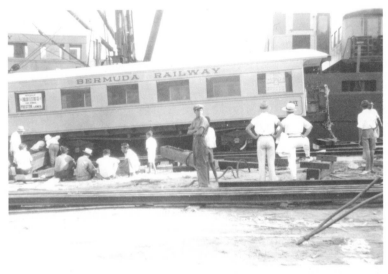

Two views of rolling stock being unloaded form the *SS Barbarian* in Hamilton Harbour. The notices in the motor coach's windows in the lower picture are of interest: the left hand one is merely an "advertisement" for English Electric, but the right had one shows weight and dimensions data for load distribution purposes.

A memorable day in Bermuda's railway history. Watched by Mrs Gladys Kitchen from the family home at Salt Kettle, Paget, the *SS Barbarian* makes her way slowly in towards the dockside of Hamilton Harbour with the first of the rolling stock. Temporary rails had been laid at the dockside to receive the vehicles.

INITIAL ROLLING STOCK

The main movement of rolling stock from England, where it had been built at the English Electric Company's Dick Kerr Tramworks at Preston, was on the SS *Barbarian*, which arrived on 2nd September 1931, and the SS *Norwegian* which docked on 7th January 1932 (after the line had been opened).

The railway's primary rolling stock consisted of:

        6 Motor Coaches, numbered 10 to 15.
        2 Motor Freight Locomotives, numbered 30 and 31.
        2 Double Motor Truck Locomotives, numbered 100 and 101.
        6 1st Class Chair Cars ("Pullmans").
        2 Trailer Freight Vans (Box Cars).
        6 Covered Passenger Cars ("Toast Racks").
        1 "Planet" Contractors Loco.
        1 Motorised Inspection Speeder
        1 Oil Tank Wagon, 1 Flat Car and 2 Open Wagons

Fuller details of the rolling stock are at Appendix A.

When, finally, all the work was completed, the 80 or so staff to be employed had been signed-on and the great day of opening approached, the bill for the construction of the line and aquisition of rolling stock had come to over one million pounds - making the Bermuda Railway probably the most expensive ever built in terms of "cost per track mile". It was also one of the slowest, in "track miles per year" terms, yet by Bermuda timescales this was hardly surprising - as it took 21 years to plan, tender for and build the first causeway to St George's Island and 14 years for the Watford bridge to reach fruition from first being approved!

Typical of the rural scenery through which the line ran, this view shows the track curving gently below the hill upon which Gibb's Hill Lighthouse stands - between Black Bay Sidings and Lighthouse Station. The gap in the sleepers is where Southampton Parish Tribe Road 2 crosses the railway's right of way.

THE LINE IS OPENED

On Saturday 31st October 1931 - Gladys Kitchen's birthday! - the Governor of Bermuda, Lieutenant General Sir Thomas Cubitt performed the opening formalities for the western section of the line. Following a ceremony beside No 1 Shed in Front Street, Hamilton, Lady Cubitt started the first car and it pulled away towards Somerset. Approaching Ridell's Bay Station a problem was encountered with the brakes and it was found necessary to leave the troublesome coach behind in the passing loop.

Large crowds gather in Front Street, Hamilton on "Opening Day" to see the first official train depart for Somerset. The shop facades today still bear a remarkable similarity to those pictured here on 31st October 1931.

At Bridge Hill Station, amid due pomp and circumstance and with General Manager Mr Ronald Stemp and Chief Engineer Mr Harold Kitchen in attendance, Sir Thomas cut a ribbon across the permanent way and the "Special" continued across the high bridge towards its destination - where Miss Rosemary Grissel, Lady Cubitt's daughter, drove in a ceremonial last spike.

The official opening ceremony at Somerset Bridge. The Colony's
Governor, Lieutenant General Sir Thomas Cubitt, cuts the tape at
the eastern end of the bridge. The train is actually standing at
Bridge Hill Station, the nameboard for which can just be seen
behind the two gentlemen in dark suits on Sir Thomas's right.

Seven weeks later, on 19th December and with
considerably less ceremony, the section of line from
Hamilton to St George was opened, the first passenger
train leaving Front Street at 2.30 pm. The Bermuda
Railway was up and running!

Smartly attired travellers alight at Aquarium Station
on the occasion of the station's official opening in 1937.

THE WORKING YEARS

For the first couple of months of operation the eastern section of line operated only a limited service, but the railway soon settled down into a regular routine and provided a good and well-used service for native Bermudians and visitors alike. Each weekday saw large numbers of the servants of commerce and industry travelling to and from work in Hamilton and, to a much lesser extent St George, at classic "rush hour" times, many bringing with them the bicycles they needed for transport to and from their nearest railway station. Getting bikes on and especially off the coaches was always a problem, particularly when it came to untangling the mass of handlebars, saddles, pedals and chains that almost always resulted from trying to pack too many cycles into too small a space. In fact, one of the most common repair jobs at the East Broadway Works was the making good of coachwork damaged by the cycles!

Crossing Flatts Bridge in May 1941 with, in the top right hand corner of the photograph, Flatts West Trestle also visible. Note the telephone wires suspended alongside the timber approach work and the refuges on either side of the track.

At weekends the railway provided the means for folk to get around the islands to visit relatives and friends whilst, of course, there were always the revenue-earning tourists to take to the many beauty spots of Bermuda. Legislation required a number of the trains each day to operate at lower "statuatory fare" prices.

Ever mindful of the tourist market, the Railway Company issued a booklet *"Seeing the Sights by Railway"*, telling of the attractions offered at a variety of stops, such as:

"PROSPECT STATION....where Parade service at 10 o'clock on Sunday morning is a never-failing lure for visitors."

"AQUARIUM....a five minute walk up a colorful road to the unrivalled Government Aquarium. There are twenty-seven tanks containing over 200 species of fish taken from Bermuda waters."

"BAILEY'S BAY....the Crystal and Leamington Caves. These caves are a wonder of nature, and they have an enchanting atmosphere which will recall the fairy tales of your youth. .....Out to sea is the hulk of the "Shah", last steam-and-sail battleship of the British navy."

"MULLET BAY, the graveyard of many a once-noble ship."

"KHYBER PASS is fittingly named after the famous Pass in India. A few yards from the track the narrow road is hewn through a high cliff, making a ravine of great beauty."

"EVANS BAY is the centre of Bermuda's agricultural section, and practically all of the produce destined for U.S. and Canada is shipped from here."

"SOMERSET terminus, a quiet and rural town with lovely walks and charming houses. .... Luncheons and refreshments are served at Frith's Bar, Mangrove Bay Hotel, Summerside Hotel, The Beaches, The Cedars, and The Cambridge."

The booklet concludes with the words

"Travel the restful way in the Isles of Rest"

Until the spectre of war in Europe and the Far East darkened the horizon, the railway led an unremarkable existence. Early problems were encountered with vandalism, which was put down to disgruntled horse-drawn carriage drivers, but these were soon a thing of the past; occasionally cows would wander on to the tracks, requiring an emergency stop from the drivers, but the safety record was excellent - especially when the proximity of trains and pedestrians and horses in Front Street is taken into account - and no directly attributable in-service fatalities are recorded (although a docker had been fatally injured during one of the unloading operations at dockside in 1931).

The social side of railway life in the mid-1930s - the Bermuda Railway soccer team poses for the camera. The player marked by a cross is Conductor Stanley Acton (whose daughter kindly lent me this photograph). The Company also had a drama troup, who called themselves "The Railway Rascals".

In the early 1930s a major programme of sleeper and rail replacement was embarked upon and a schedule of bridge and trestle painting enacted. Harold Kitchen's capable staff kept the rolling stock in tip top condition, although the remoteness of Bermuda from the Drewry Works in England led to some excellent examples of initiative and improvisation.

POST CARDS

Views of Bermuda featuring the railway were always popular.

The top card, possibly the best known of all the "railway post cards", shows a train proceeding across the Bailey's Bay Trestle; the lower "Kodak Photo Post Card" portrays a rather grubby No 10 standing with a "toast rack" at Hamilton (Cenotaph) Station.

THE END DRAWS NEAR

WORLD WAR II

Bermuda was to make an important contribution to the
Allied cause in the 1939-45 War, with the opening of
the US Naval Base in April 1941 being particularly
significant. As part of the Military Lend Lease
arrangements, control of the land for the bases was
handed over by the British Government to that of the
United States, in return for military supplies -
foremost amongst which were a number of First World War
vintage 4-stack destroyers.

Supporting the War Effort - a train at Riddell's Bay Station carrying construction
materials for the military bases. Second from the right stands the man who will
always be associated with the Bermuda Railway as long as it is talked about: Mr
Harold Jennings Kitchen - Chief Engineer 1931 to 1947, and heavily involved in
the design and construction of the railway and, then, Director of Public
Transportation from 1947 until his early, untimely death in 1950.

From the base's Kindley Field aerodrome, long range
maritime patrol aircraft ranged far and wide in the
hunt for Axis submarines, whilst surface escort vessels
called for emergency repairs and occasional
rebunkering. The island achieved importance as the main
censorship station for trans-Atlantic mails.

The railway supported the war effort admirably, particularly in carrying troops and supplies from dockside to the main US base on St David's Island and to the Annex near George's Bay - large parts of both of these military facilities being built on land reclaimed from the sea - and during the construction phases of which the measured gauge clearances of some of the cuttings and, especially, the tunnel below Par-La-Ville Gardens were strained to the absolute limit. Resident British military personnel also made good use of the railway, both on and off duty. Over 1,500,000 fare-paying passengers were carried in 1945 (the most in any one year), but even this did not allow the company to break even financially - let alone show a profit!

Military personnel made good use of the railway in their off-duty hours. Here a train stands ready to depart from Somerset, packed with Royal Navy sailors eager to "hit the town". Note the upright rail section in the foreground - used to carry the signalling system telephone wires, and still occasionally to be found at station sites today.

Because of the overriding importance of the war effort, the restrictions imposed under the 1908 Motor Car Act were dramatically eased, and official motor vehicles of all shapes, sizes and types were allowed on to the island's narrow roads - a foretaste of what was to come after the abolition of The Act. The railway faced the problem of the lack of manpower, as well as of spares - and reading today of the attitude of officialdom towards the Railway Company, when it sought to increase marginally its staff, one could be forgiven for imaging that the Government was on a different side in the war to the Company (which was striving to improve its support of military operations). Only a relatively low priority was given to the loading of railway spares into ships destined to battle their way across the Atlantic to Bermuda, so the extra workload called for by the military authorities, and the lack of essential maintenance, led to a marked rundown in the efficiency of the whole operation. The increase in use by the military, but the lack of spares and ability to carry out essential repaior works, revealed the War's effect upon Bermuda and its railway to be very much in the nature of a mixed blessing. Additionally, before the war was two years old, the first signs of the rot that was becoming widespread in the timbers of the wooden trestles became apparent to the Management. As an indication of how serious the problems to be encountered in the years ahead were expected to be, the General Manager (Ronald Stemp) resigned - without forewarning - from his position whilst on a business trip to the USA in December 1942!

A British serviceman cycles along Pitt's Bay Road as a passenger train eases its way into the Richmond Road Tunnel, Hamilton.

- 21 -

In an effort to improve the tractive power available for not only the heavy military loads but services in general, two further locomotives were imported in 1942 and 1943 from the USA. These "Cummins Diesels" - as they were always known - were, unlike the Drewry locomotives, diesel-electric powered. For further details see Appendix A.

THE POST-WAR YEARS

By the time that peace returned to Bermuda, the railway portrayed a sorry picture, which was not helped by the 1946 abolition of Motor Car Act; by the end of that year, 352 private cars, 144 taxis and 426 commercial vehicles were already registered and a major programme of road improvements was in hand. The first bus service, Hamilton to Tuckers Town, ran on 23rd April.

East Broadway yard in 1947. No 13 stands "on shed", with a "toast rack" passenger carriage on the right and four flat wagons, loaded with a variety of steel girders, on the left. The structure visible above the third flat wagon is the high pressure wash water pump.

The Railway Company could see that the writing was on the wall; faced with massive repair bills and an ever decreasing number of passengers to be carried, it applied to the Government to be bought out. The Railway

Purchase Act and its associated Operation of the Bermuda Railway Act, were approved at the beginning of 1946, and on Sunday 26th January the railway passed from private into public ownership. (A Sunday was chosen as changeover day in order that all staff could be paid by the Railway Company up to a Saturday as usual!)

For the £115,000 that it paid for the Company, "plus a duly calculated proportion of all insurances, office and telephone rent and truck licence duty paid in advance", the Government aquired "The whole of the railway undertaking of the Company, including all lands and buildings and appurtenances thereto belonging and all works, and (save and except book debts and cash) all other property and assets". The Government paid into the coffers of the new public body £15,000 as working capital and appointed in charge Mr Harold Kitchen previously, of course, the Chief Engineer.

The vast amount of timber, even in the composite construction of Flatts Bridge and Flatts West Trestle is readily apparent in this view across Flatts Inlet from Flatts Station. It was the widespread timber decay in structures such as these that hastened the end of the railway.

On 22nd March, the Transport Control Board appointed consulting engineers Sanborn & Fitzpatrick of New York to carry out a complete survey of the railway system. They found the wooden trestles, despite the repairs that had been carried out on them in the war years when materials were in such short supply, to be in very poor condition; over 85% of the timbers showing some sort of decay. It became apparent that the timbers had been pressure treated with preservative before being shipped out from England, but only in random lengths, and when field cut to size in Bermuda for the trestles, that the ends had neither been properly capped nor treated with sufficient preservative. Wind, waves, rain and spray had all taken their toll!

The consultants estimated that repairs to the bridges, sleepers and track alone, with indirect fees, would be $306,000; to put the whole railway back into first class condition was estimated at $850,000, whilst conversion of the railway trackbed to highway would cost $1,819,000 (and achieve very little).

Meanwhile the railway struggled on. In 1946 alone Harold Kitchen's private diary reveals 182 major breakdowns away from the workshops (ie: one every other day), and he writes:

> Monday March 4th - "Muddled Through".
> Sunday 9th June - "Real Bad Day".
> Saturday 22nd June - "10, 13, 14, 15, 100 and 201 all U/S."

During 1947, under 41% of the 1945 number of passengers was carried and, rather than pay out the vast sum required to bring the railway back to peak efficiency again, the decision was made to abandon the system.

The replacement bus system was advanced enough for the line out to Somerset to be abandoned on 1st January 1948 and at midnight Miss Grissel, who had driven in the last spike in October 1931, pulled out the very same spike and dismantling operations got under way. Today this spike, engraved, silver plated and mounted on a Bermuda Cedar block, is in the possession of Canadian railway historian Raymond Corley.

Because preparations for the bus service to St George were not so advanced (the road contouring and strengthening was incomplete and many of the initial

order of 28 motor buses still had to reach Bermuda),
the eastern section of line continued working into the
spring, but only as far as the Richmond Road, and the
very last service train ran in Bermuda on 1st May 1948.
The Bermuda Railway was no more!

Perhaps one of the most bitter twists of irony was the
fact that Harold Kitchen, who had given so much to the
railway from its very earliest days, was appointed
Director of Public Transport; salt was added to the
wound by the choice of the site of the East Broadway
(Middle Road) Railway Yard as the main bus depot.
Sadly, Mr Kitchen's heart was never in the new
transport system, and he passed away in 1950 with the
railway still his first love. Never had a railway had a
better servant or supporter!

An undated view of Aquarium Station - looking in the direction of Hamilton -
showing clearly the passing loop and, in the foreground, the spring-operated
points (switch gear). The station building now houses the Bermuda Railway Museum.

Although the investors in the Bermuda Railway never
received a penny in dividends for their support of the
project, and although the line operate for less than
seventeen years, it passed into history with a fine
record: during its commercial days, it had safely
carried over fourteen million passengers during good

weather and bad, in daylight and the darkness, and in peace and war. Despite the shortcomings in its autumnal years, it had provided a great and good-value service to the people of Bermuda - "The Old Rattle and Shake", as it was locally known, will long be remembered with affection.

Two final indignities! Demolition work taking place on the Richmond Road Tunnel - this view being of the Pitts Bay Road portal (where the Harold Haye Frith Building now stands), and redundant rolling stock laid up at the Yard prior to disposal.

THE BRITISH GUIANA CONNECTION

The first railway system to built on the Continent of South America was that in the colony of British Guiana. It consisted of 61 miles of standard gauge track - the East Coast Railway from Georgetown to Rosignol (opposite ew Amsterdam, the colony's second town, on the estuary of the Berbice River) - and 19 miles of 3'6" gauge track - the West Coast Railway from Vreeden-Hoop to Parika. As in Bermuda, the building of the railway was a slow process, and one indication of its problems was the failure of the special (silver plated?) spade and wheel barrow ordered from England to arrive in time for the first official opening ceremony when the standard gauge railway reached its first objective - the community and sugar plantation at Mahaies, 21½ miles from Georgetown. Operating from 1848 as The Demerara Railway, the system was taken over by the British Guiana Government on 1st January 1922 under the control of the Colonial Transport Department - which also operated the local fleet of coastal and ferry steam ships.

Waiting passengers and the station buildings complete
this rural scene on the outskirts of Georgetown.

In addition to the two public lines, there were at least two other narrow gauge lines - both of which served the mineral extraction and sugar industries in the more remote regions of the country.

Not only did the war take its toll on the Bermuda Railway: down in South America that in British Guiana was also suffering similar strains. For example, in their annual Transport and Harbour Department Report to the Governor for the year of 1943, the Commissioners stated "We have found it necessary to curtail further the number of train services on the East Coast Railway owing to the difficulties there would be in replacing rolling stock in the event of it becoming necessary to do so, and in obtaining the necessary supplies of patent fuel, coal and wood fuel to maintain the usual services. Considerable difficulty has been experienced in maintaining locomotive power, due to the fact that five locomotive boilers ordered have not yet been received." As far back as in 1930, the railway system's Managing Director had described portions of both his passenger coaches and his freight wagons as being "of ancient design". Also at that time, a loco imported in 1863 was described as "still doing good work"!

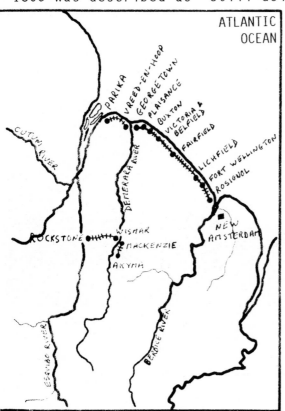

ATLANTIC OCEAN

Gauge and Distance Data

Georgetown to Rosignol: 4'8½" (Standard) - 60 miles.

Vreed-En-Hoop to Parika: 3'6" - 20 miles.

Wismar to Rockstone: 1 metre - 20 miles.

Mackenzie to Akyma: 2'6" - 12 miles.

Sketch Map of the British Guiana Railway System in the 1930s.

In 1944 the railway had obtained, as surplus to military requirements, two petrol locos, and six 30-ton wagons from the US War Department - the locos being particularly needed to operate special trains carrying milk from the hinterland to the City of Georgetown. This alone was not enough to operate the railway at the level of service required, and when it became known that the Bermuda Government wished to dispose of its own railway, an approach was made to aquire it "lock, stock and barrel" for an agreed sum between the two Colonial Governments of $414,000 BWI (British West Indian Dollars)/£86,000 sterling as part of a 10-year renewal programme. (In British Guiana a government sponsored study to see if the way ahead lay with the train or the lorry had come down in favour of the former - the opposite result to that obtained in the same exercise in Bermuda.) About 150 lengths of rail were left behind in Bermuda, considered too rusty for further railway use and, together with the steel bridge components, were sold for scrap: almost everything else of value made the journey south.

Laden with Bermuda Railway equipment, the Lamport & Holt Lines *M/V Sheridan* makes her way through The Great Sound en-route to Georgetown, British Guiana.

On 13th August 1948 the *Sheridan* docked in Georgetown with the first equipment from Bermuda, followed in turn

by the *Dominic*, *Jutahy* and *Pachetoa*. All items were
received safely, despite difficulty in unloading, and
the two diesel locos, two of the motor coaches and a
number of passenger coaches were in service before the
end of the year - augmenting the 16 steam and 7 petrol
locos already operating, and 32 passenger carriages, 16
other coaching vehicles and 293 goods and service
wagons. The ubiquitous Harold Kitchen supervised the
initial starting-in-service of the new aquisitions.
Under the auspices of Lieutenant Colonel R V Tears, the
General Manager in British Guiana (who had earlier
visit Bermuda to supervise the collection of the items
purchased), the coaches were reconditioned, painted red
and fitted with larger windows, new seats and
washrooms; one coach was turned into an observation car
for The Governor, complete with refrigerator and
kitchenette. The diesel locos were painted green, The
signalling equipment, general stores and lengths of
rail were soon put to good use, and during 1949 alone
3,262 of the pine sleepers from Bermuda were freshly
creosted and used to replace mora (a local hardwood)
sleepers at the end of their useful life.

The *M/V Sheridan* alongside the wharf at Georgetown Harbour, prior to unloading
the deck cargo - but with temporary rails already in position to carry the new
aquisitions away. The locos are 100 or 101 (left) and a "Series 10".

At the same time, not related to the Bermuda equipment, the railway was undergoing a conversion programme of the steam locomotives, from coal to oil-burning.

Carrying the number 41, and resplendent in a dark green livery similar that of British Railways "Southern Suburban Green" and Mercury motifs, one of the ex-Bermuda Railway motor coaches stands at Georgetown Terminus in 1952. Note, following the British practice, that the "non-1st class accommodation" is designated as 3rd, and not as 2nd class.

Being standard gauge, the Bermuda Railway stock was only employed on the main line between Georgetown, the capital, and Rosignol - with its passenger and goods ferry connection to New Amsterdam. The intergration of the new stock into the Guyana system, and an increase by three of the station passing loops provided, led to a marked improvement in the service on offer - with a commendable 20 mph average speed, including stops, being achieved for the first time ever. In 1953, for example, 1,772,954 passengers were carried (total for both public lines), with peak periods of travel being in the mornings and evenings as workers and school children made their way to and from the capital.

In addition to the passenger service it offered, the railway played an important part in the colony's economy life - carrying goods and materials (92,769 tons in 1953) such as sugar, rum and a wide range of foodstuffs from the plantations and farms and supplying

In this evocative view of railway activity outside Georgetown Terminus in 1952, an ex-Bermuda Railway motor freight van stands facing one of the Guiana Railway's Sharp-Stewart tank locos - beyond the tall funnel of which can be seen an ex-Bermuda Railway "Pullman" passenger coach and trailer freight van.

these same establishments with manufactured goods, coal, fertilizers and the like. There were 15 stations on this line, and traffic management was by a central control for the first 20 miles out of Georgetown and by a staff system for the rest of the route.

Amongst this sad line of elderly rolling stock standing on an overgrown siding in the Guiana countryside in 1952, and presumably awaiting scrapping, can be seen two of the ex-Bermuda Railway "toast rack" passenger coaches.

An ambitious plan to construct a railway from Guiana to Brazil never came to fruition - mainly because of the heavy country it would have had to traverse and the rapid advance of air travel - and today, like Bermuda, the Co-operative Republic of Guyana has no public railway system - both the coastal lines having been taken out of service in 1972.

The large Central Station still stands in Georgetown but, except where they were set in tarmac road surfaces, all the public standard and 3'6" gauge rails have now been lifted. There is, however, still an industrial line serving the Guyana Mining Enterprise, which runs between Linden, Ituni and Coomacka in the country's North West District.

Georgetown Station today. The permanent way to Rosignol ran out from the right of the terminus, (as seen from this position).

THE BERMUDA TRAIL

A small part of the trackbed had been Tarmaced as a cycle track as early as 1952, but it was not kept in good condition and drew much criticism from the public - even meriting a caustic editorial article in *The Royal Gazette*.

In 1962 a Mr Frank Gosling proposed a double track, narrow gauge line along the old trackbed, but this never progressed from the speculative stage. Imagine just how great a tourist attraction that would have been in the 1990s!

Finally in 1984, as part of the celebrations to commemorate the 375th anniversary of Bermuda's discovery by Sir George Somers, 18 miles of the trackbed was dedicated as *The Railway Trail*. The public notice to announce this event appears overleaf, and full details of the line's status and use today can be found in Chapter 5.

BERMUDA
RAILWAY TRAIL

GRAND OPENING
SUNDAY, JUNE 9th

The first four sections of the Railway Trail

from Paget to Sandys will be opened by the Minister of Works and
Housing at two ceremonies — the first at WARWICK SECONDARY
SCHOOL at 2 p.m., the second at WHITE HILL FIELD at 4 p.m.

Join Quinton Edness and local dignitaries at the Warwick
Secondary School ceremony and walk with them to White Hill Field
for the second ceremony.

In addition, groups of young people representing youth
organizations will be walking the trail. Join them at South Road Roundabout at 12.15 p.m.
to walk the trail to Warwick, or at Beacon Hill Bus Terminal, Sandys, at 2.45 p.m. to
walk to White Hill.

Please take care at all road crossings.

T I C K E T S ,   F A R E S
a n d   T I M E T A B L E S

Currencies: Bermuda Railway fares were, naturally, based on the British Imperial money system - pounds, shillings and pence (£.s.d). I have placed the current, metric, sterling equivalent against the "old" fares in brackets, eg: 5/- (25p).

To convert the fares **very approximately** to their modern day US/Bermuda dollar equivalent, double this latter figure, eg: 4/- (20p) = 40 cents.

TICKETS

Today, when railways generally use electronic, computer-based ticketing systems, it is refreshing to take a look at the system used by The Bermuda Railway Company right up until two years before its demise.

The system was based upon that used in the UK for the recording of fares paid for a variety of services: mainly for railways, buses and trams, but also for fairground rides, admission to public gardens and piers, and the hire of deck chairs, etc - and utilised the Bell Punch System, patented by The Bell Punch & Printing Co Ltd, of London, England.

The system consisted of disposable, pre-printed tickets, on which was shown, basically, the fare paid and the stations between which it was valid. Each denomination of ticket was an exclusive colour and was serial numbered. The tickets were supplied in stapled bundles of 100, and were carried on a linear clip rack containing enough tickets to service the route covered.

Each ticket was divided so that the adjacent stage titles were spaced apart by the value of the ticket denomination. For example, Hamilton to Richmond Road on, say, a 1/6 (7½p) ticket would be next to Tennis Court on a 2/- (10p) ticket. Thus a hole punched through at Hamilton on the 1/6 ticket would read Richmond Road on the reverse side - the destination beyond which the ticket ceased to be valid; if punched at the same place (Hamilton) on the

2/- ticket, the ticket was valid as far as Tennis Court Station. So, the conductor selected a ticket of the value for the distance the passenger wished to travel, punched a hole in it at the name of the station at which the person embarked - and, on the reverse side, the hole indicated the station at which the passenger should alight.

With the conductor going about his duties in the background, Inspector MacCudden examines the tickets of passengers in "Pullman" 21 - during the visit of the Anatole Vilzak-American School of Ballet to Bermuda in the winter of 1938-39.

The chronium plated Bell Punch, itself, and the money pouch were mounted on individual straps hung from the conductor's right and left shoulders, around the neck, with the punch located at the left hip and the money pouch at the right. The conductors uniform consisted of grey jacket and trousers, with green piping and vertical green stripe respectively, worn over a grey shirt and green tie and topped by a grey peaked cap. Uniform shoes were of black leather.

(One the subject of uniforms, inspectors differed from conductors by having 2 sleeve bands instead of one. A driver's uniform was navy blue, with a brass insignia "BRC" on his visor cap.)

Taken on the North Shore, this photograph shows clearly the uniforms of a driver and conductor. Note, particularly, the conductor's chronium plated Bell Punch, shoulder straps, and money pouch.

The locomotives are both of the first delivery "10 series".

The wearing of the punch and pouch, and the carrying of the ticket rack, were considered to be the conductor's "tokens of office" and assisted him, in an abstract way, in maintaining order on the trains.

With the ticket rack being held in the left hand, the appropriate ticket was extracted with the other hand and inserted in the Bell Punch machine, where the conductor punched the hole in the appropriate ticket by pulling down the operating lever with his thumb. As the lever was pulled down a high pitched bell (hence the name) operated to indicate that the operation was being legally performed; if there was no ticket between the punch lips, the lever would not operate and the bell would not sound.

To reconcile the conductor's takings at the end of a duty, the body of the ticket machine would be opened with a special stylus and the ticket punchings counted according to their colours - the colours indicating the ticket denominations. Float plus tickets issued to the conductor, less tickets remaining, ticket punchings and cash handed in should be the same!

Although London Transport soldiered on with the Bell Punch system until 1953, the system was superseded in Bermuda - just 2 years before the line closed - by one using a hand held printer activated by a crank handle on its side. The ticket issued was rather similar to one from a shop's till, and was printed individually with details of each transaction.

FARES

The fare system was anything but simple.

As the timetables which follow indicate, statutory fares - often known in the UK as "workmen's fares" - applied on certain of the services. With first and second class non-statutory fares, the statutory fares and, initially, 15 different fare stages - 30 possible prices applied (with a corresponding similar number of ticket denominations). Additionally, of course, there were free pass holders and other concessionary fares! The Bermuda Railway's conductors certainly had to have their wits about them.

Nevertheless, considering how high was the cost of building the railway, the fares were very reasonable; typical examples of single journey early-1930s fares, from Hamilton, were:

To	1st Class	2nd Class	Statutory
Aquarium, or Lighthouse	1/8 (8½p)	1/3 (6p)	1/- (5p)
Bailey's Bay or Somerset Bridge	2/4 (11½p)	1/9 (9p)	1/2 (5½p)
St George	3/4 (16½p)	2/6 (12½p)	1/8 (13½p)
Somerset	4/- (20p)	3/- (15p)	2/- (10p)

TIMETABLES

With the passage of time, as elsewhere in the world, the Bermuda service schedule was subject to revision; the tables that follow on the next pages represent the timetable as it existed in 1939, except that I have shown the time by the internationally used 24 hour clock. Further trains - Tourist Specials, Boat Trains, Freight Trains, Maintenance Trains, etc - ran as required.

HAMILTON to ST GEORGE

Notes:

♦ = Sunday excepted; ▾ = Statutory Fares apply;

∞ = Statutory Fares apply on Saturdays only;

☼ = Open daylight hours only (times shown during dark hours are passing times only).

	♦▾	♦▾	♦▾			▾			▾	▾			∞		
Hamilton	0615	0700	0845	1012	1130	1226	1332	1453	1612	1730	1825	2003	2120	2310	0020
Queen Street	0616	0701	0846	1013	1131	1227	1337	1454	1613	1731	1826	2004	2121	2311	0021
Bermudiana	0619	0704	0849	1016	1134	1230	1336	1457	1616	1734	1829	2007	2124	2314	0024
Serpentine	0621	0706	0851	1018	1136	1232	1338	1459	1618	1736	1831	2009	2126	2316	0026
Tennis Stadium	0623	0708	0853	1020	1138	1234	1340	1501	1620	1738	1833	2011	2128	2318	0028
Racecourse	0625	0710	0855	1022	1140	1236	1342	1503	1622	1740	1835	2013	2130	2320	0030
Pond Hill	0627	0712	0857	1024	1142	1238	1344	1505	1624	1742	1837	2015	2132	2322	0032
Prospect	0629	0714	0859	1026	1144	1240	1346	1507	1626	1744	1839	2017	2134	2324	0034
Devonshire	0632	0717	0902	1029	1147	1243	1349	1510	1629	1747	1842	2020	2137	2327	0037
Store Hill	0636	0721	0906	1033	1151	1247	1353	1514	1633	1751	1846	2024	2141	2331	0041
Flatts	0640	0725	0910	1037	1155	1251	1357	1518	1637	1755	1850	2028	2145	2335	0045
Aquarium	0641	0726	0911	1038	1156	1252	1358	1519	1638	1756	1851	2029	2146	2336	0046
Shelly Bay	0644	0729	0914	1041	1159	1255	1401	1522	1641	1759	1854	2032	2149	2339	0049
Crawl	0647	0732	0917	1044	1202	1258	1404	1525	1644	1802	1857	2035	2152	2342	0052
Bayley's Bay	0654	0739	0924	1051	1209	1305	1411	1532	1651	1809	1904	2042	2159	2349	0059
Coney Island	0657	0742	0927	1054	1212	1308	1414	1535	1654	1812	1907	2045	2204	2354	0104
Ferry Point	0659	0744	0929	1056	1214	1310	1416	1537	1656	1814	1909	2047	2204	2354	0104
Oil Dock	0705	0750	0935	1102	1220	1316	1422	1543	1702	1820	1915	2053	2210	0000	0110
☼ Mullet Bay	0707	0752	0937	1104	1222	1318	1424	1545	1704	1822	1917	2053	2212	0002	0112
Wellington	0709	0754	0939	1106	1224	1320	1426	1547	1706	1824	1919	2057	2214	0004	0114
St George	0710	0755	0940	1107	1225	1321	1427	1548	1707	1825	1920	2058	2215	0005	0115

An additional train ran on Saturday and Sunday evenings only, leaving Hamilton at 2003 and arriving at St George at 2058.

Tourist Ticket for use on the Eastern Arm of the Railway. Note that St George has been printed with an "s" at the end: once with and once without an apostrophe!

ST GEORGE to HAMILTON

Notes:

♦ = Sunday excepted; ▼ = Statutory Fares apply;

✿ = Open daylight hours only (times shown during dark hours are passing times only).

	♦▼	♦▼	♦	♦							▼		▼
St George	0550	0800	0905	1020	1140	1250	1340	1505	1615	1740	1850	2010	0010
Wellington	0551	0801	0906	1021	1141	1251	1341	1506	1616	1741	1851	2011	0011
✿ Mullet Bay	0553	0803	0908	1023	1143	1253	1343	1508	1618	1743	1853	----	----
Oil Dock	0555	0805	0910	1025	1145	1255	1345	1510	1620	1745	1855	2015	0015
Ferry Point	0601	0811	0916	1031	1151	1301	1351	1516	1626	1751	1901	2021	0021
Coney Island	0603	0813	0918	1033	1153	1303	1353	1518	1628	1753	1903	2023	0026
Bayley's Bay	0606	0816	0921	1036	1156	1306	1356	1521	1631	1756	1906	2026	0026
Crawl	0613	0823	0928	1043	1203	1313	1403	1528	1638	1803	1913	2033	0033
Shelly Bay	0616	0826	0931	1046	1203	1313	1406	1531	1641	1806	1916	2036	0036
Aquarium	0619	0829	0934	1049	1209	1319	1409	1534	1644	1809	1919	2039	0036
Flatts	0620	0830	0935	1050	1210	1320	1410	1535	1645	1810	1920	2040	0044
Store Hill	0624	0834	0939	1054	1214	1324	1414	1539	1649	1814	1924	2044	0044
Devonshire	0628	0838	0943	1058	1218	1328	1418	1543	1653	1818	1928	2048	0048
Prospect	0631	0841	0946	1101	1221	1331	1421	1546	1656	1821	1931	2051	0051
Pond Hill	0633	0843	0948	1103	1223	1333	1423	1548	1658	1823	1933	2053	0053
Racecourse	0635	0845	0950	1105	1225	1335	1425	1550	1700	1825	1935	2055	0055
Tennis Stadium	0637	0847	0952	1107	1227	1337	1427	1552	1702	1827	1937	2057	0057
Serpentine	0639	0849	0954	1109	1229	1339	1429	1554	1704	1829	1939	2059	0059
Bermudiana	0641	0851	0956	1111	1231	1341	1431	1556	1706	1831	1941	2101	0101
Queen Street	0644	0854	0959	1114	1234	1344	1434	1559	1709	1834	1944	2104	0104
Hamilton	0645	0855	1000	1115	1235	1345	1435	1600	1710	1835	1945	2105	0105

Additional trains ran on Sunday mornings only at 0950 and on Saturday and Sunday evenings at 2105, arriving at Hamilton 55 minutes later.

Pre-printed 6d (2½p) ticket, coloured buff, for the carriage of a dog, bicycle or perambulator.

HAMILTON to SOMERSET

Notes:

♣ = Saturdays & Sundays excepted; ♦ = Sunday excepted;

▲ = Terminated at Evan's Bay Monday to Saturday.

▼ = Statutory Fares apply;

∞ = Statutory Fares apply on Saturdays only;

☼ = Open daylight hours only (times shown during dark hours are passing times only).

◄ = Not an official passenger stop.

	♦▼	♦▼	▲		▼		▼	▼	♣	∞
Hamilton	0623	0808	1000	1118	1240	1440	1600	1715	1840	2138	2325
Middle Road	0627	0812	1004	1122	1244	1444	1604	1719	1844	2142	2329
Hospital	0631	0816	1008	1126	1248	1448	1608	1723	1848	2146	2333
Rural Hill	0633	0818	1010	1128	1250	1450	1610	1725	1850	2148	2335
Elbow Beach	0635	0820	1012	1130	1252	1452	1612	1727	1852	2150	2337
Ord Road	0637	0822	1014	1132	1254	1454	1614	1729	1854	2152	2339
Cobb's Hill	0640	0825	1017	1135	1257	1457	1617	1732	1875	2155	2342
Belmont	0643	0828	1020	1138	1300	1500	1620	1735	1900	2158	2345
Khyber Pass	0645	0830	1022	1140	1302	1502	1622	1737	1902	2200	2347
Riddell's Bay	0649	0834	1026	1144	1306	1506	1626	1741	1906	2204	2351
Lighthouse	0654	0839	1031	1149	1311	1511	1631	1746	1911	2209	2356
◄ Black Bay	0656	0841	1033	1151	1313	1513	1633	1748	1913	2211	2358
Church Road	0659	0844	1036	1154	1316	1516	1636	1751	1916	2214	0001
Frank's Bay	0702	0847	1039	1157	1319	1519	1639	1754	1919	2217	0004
Evan's Bay	0704	0849	1041	1159	1321	5121	1641	1756	1921	2219	0006
☼ George's Bay	0708	0853		1203	1325	1525	1645	1800	1925	2223	0010
White Hill	0710	0855		1205	1327	1527	1647	1802	1927	2225	0012
☼ Bridge Hill	0712	0857		1207	1329	1529	1649	1804	1929	2227	0014
Somerset Bridge	0713	0858		1208	1330	1530	1650	1805	1930	2228	0015
Sound View Road	0718	0903		1213	1335	1535	1655	1810	1935	2233	0020
Scott's Hill Rd	0719	0904		1214	1336	1536	1656	1811	1936	2234	0021
Broom Street	0720	0905		1215	1337	1537	1657	1812	1937	2235	0022
Somerset	0721	0906		1216	1338	1538	1658	1813	1938	2236	0023

Additional trains ran on Saturday and Sunday evenings at 2105 and 2205, arriving at Hamilton 58 minutes later.

SOMERSET to HAMILTON

Notes:

♦ = Sunday excepted; ▼ = Statutory Fares apply;

✿ = Open daylight hours only (times shown during dark hours are passing times only).

◄ = Not an official passenger stop.

	♦▼	♦▼	♦	♦	▼			▼	▼		
Somerset	0600	0745	0915		1230	1350	1625	1725	1900	2020	2320
Broom Street	0601	0746	0916		1231	1351	1626	1726	1901	2021	2321
Scott's Hill Rd	0602	0747	0917		1232	1352	1627	1727	1902	2022	2322
Sound View Road	0603	0748	0918		1233	1353	1628	1728	1903	2023	2323
Somerset Bridge	0608	0753	0923		1238	1358	1633	1733	1908	2028	2328
✿ Bridge Hill	0609	0754	0924		1239	1359	1634	1734	1909	2029	2329
White Hill	0611	0756	0926		1241	1401	1636	1736	1911	2031	2331
✿ George's Bay	0613	0758	0928		1243	1403	1638	1738	1913	2033	2333
Evan's Bay	0617	0802	0932	1050	1247	1407	1642	1742	1917	2037	2337
Frank's Bay	0619	0804	0934	1052	1249	1409	1644	1744	1919	2039	2339
Church Road	0622	0807	0937	1055	1252	1412	1647	1747	1922	2042	2342
◄ Black Bay	0625	0810	0940	1058	1255	1415	1650	1750	1925	2045	2345
Lighthouse	0627	0812	0942	1100	1257	1417	1652	1752	1927	2047	2347
Riddell's Bay	0632	0817	0947	1105	1302	1422	1657	1757	1932	2052	2352
Khyber Pass	0636	0821	0951	1109	1306	1426	1701	1801	1936	2056	2356
Belmont	0638	0823	0953	1111	1308	1428	1703	1803	1938	2058	2358
Cobb's Hill	0641	0826	0956	1114	1311	1431	1706	1806	1941	2101	0001
Ord Road	0644	0829	0959	1117	1314	1434	1709	1809	1944	2104	0004
Elbow Beach	0646	0831	1001	1119	1316	1436	1711	1811	1946	2106	0006
Rural Hill	0648	0833	1003	1121	1318	1438	1713	1813	1948	2108	0008
Hospital	0650	0835	1005	1123	1320	1440	1715	1815	1950	2110	0010
Middle Road	0654	0839	1009	1127	1324	1444	1719	1819	1954	2114	0014
Hamilton	0658	0843	1013	1131	1328	1448	1723	1823	1958	2118	0018

Additional trains ran on Sunday mornings only at 0940 and 1125 and on Saturday and Sunday evenings at 2210, arriving at Hamilton 58 minutes later.

"A DRIVER'S LOG"

"The 5.30 pm Hamilton to St George"

Personal Recollections

by

William Kitchen

Cruise Boat Day! To the railway that meant that the passengers for the *Prince David*, moored alongside at St George's Harbour, had to be returned to their ship before sundown, whilst many of the business folk of Bermuda would be returning to their homes, in many cases complete with their bicycles, on the same train. Whilst the regular train would have been a motor coach and one chair car, on an occasion such as this one of the eight cylinder van-locomotives, a chair car and three toast racks would be required.

Locomotive No 100 had been in the running sheds all day for its "A" maintenance: bodywork examined, door locks lubricated, spark plugs and oil filters cleaned, air compressors topped up with oil, coupling and brake hoses checked, brakes, chain drives and springs all adjusted, etc. After the servicing, the loco would have been run on to the fuel stand for the yard staff to add lube oil, as required, to the engines and gearboxes, water to the cooling system and sand to the sand boxes.

Although I was employed in Bermuda on engineering duties, I was delighted when the opportunity arose for me to drive scheduled trains (Not encouraged by my father [The Chief Engineer - affectionately known to the workforce as "The Old Man"], who considered that my job was to fix'em, not drive 'em!). Today the Yard Foreman hailed me and, announcing that neither the scheduled nor the standby driver had reported for work, stated that I would have to drive "The Boat Train".

I climbed into the driving cab, and checked air tank and engine oil pressures, cooling water circulation, sander operation and the like. All was OK, so the hand brake was wound off and a toot on the air whistle (middle "C" pitch) indicated our progress away to pick up the assembled train in number 4 siding. The two coach maids jumped out just as we approached and, just two inches before the couplings met, the shunter's whistle sounded and I applied the brakes. With a gentle clank the train was connected; the air hose and electric jumpers were mated and the valves opened by the nimble shunter. The hiss of air into the train was followed by the clank of the compressor unloader control valve on the loco - followed by the "pom-pom-pom" sound of the loaded compressors.

No 100 and the Boat Train at East Broadway Yard, awaiting clearance to proceed to Hamilton (Cenotaph) Station

When the train air pipe gauge showed 75 psi, and the compressors cut out, I made a trail application and released the trailer brakes, listening for the whistle of each coach triple valve.

One bell; two, three and four bells - the shunter had checked all four coaches and all systems were "go", so off to the Middle Road Signal Cabin to pick up "the tablet" key.

The signal cabin contained two key token machines, one controlling the block section from Cobb's Hill and the other the block section to Richmond Road. The flags on both machines showed that the blocks were occupied: that would be by the 1625 ex-Somerset and the freight train returning from St George (both flags showed red, indicating "Train Coming From"). After a short wait No 31 and her freight wagons rumbled along the coral filled tracks and, the shunter having jumped out to set the switch points to enter the Middle Road Yard, stopped at the signal cabin to insert the key and clear the Richmond Road block. After I had called control on the magneto telephone, the despatcher ordered me to proceed.

The key was inserted into the token machine and turned through a quarter revolution until the green "Train Going To" flag showed, after which a further quarter revolution allowed the key to be removed and authority given to proceed into the block.

I exchanged a few "railway greetings" with the driver of No 31, removed my watch from its zoot chain and hung it on the deskstand provided - in front of a propped up copy of the timetable - and drove off down the yard out on to Front Street, crossing over the automatic, spring type exit switch points.

At the Hamilton Station, opposite the Cenotaph, a conductor for each carriage was waiting, equipped with his bell punch machine, ticket rack and money pouch. Then the fun, as always, started: the 5 o'clock rush of the locals with their bicycles. Oh, the bicycles - who could ever forget them?

"All aboard", followed by the bell of the rear chair car and off we rumbled down Front Street, with numerous blasts on the air whistle. At No 1 Shed the tourists were waiting, with cameras held high and bags full of souvenirs. One or two brave Bermudians offered up their bicycles and went to join regular travelling companions at a game of bridge already in progress in the chair car. With more bells and tooting, we slowly entered Richmond Tunnel, below the Par-La-Ville Gardens, the wheels screaming in objection to the unreasonably sharp corner on the steep up grade towards Bermudiana (Richmond Road) Station, where a blind crossing at the summit made life interesting as I watched the cyclists and horse drawn vehicles trying to beat the train.

I took the key token to the signal box and turned it in to clear the Middle Road section; the Store Hill section machine showed "Train Coming From", and soon the Hamilton-bound train ran through the spring switch to take the passing loop. After we had reported to control our respective arrivals and departures, he took the Middle Road key and I the Store Hill one, and I set off with my train down the steep grade to the blind crossing at Laffan Street, before picking up more passengers at Serpentine Road, passing though the private halt for Government House and, then drawing to a halt at Tennis Stadium Station. Passengers, many with bicycles, alighted here - and then we were off to Pond Hill, across the marshland where the Watlington Water Works was located. At Pond Hill more passengers alighted, but not so many bicycles went with them this time.

We ran on to Prospect, with no train to pass at that loop, and saw just a few passengers alight here - probably for Devonshire Dock and Bleak House - and then, after passing a deserted Devonshire Station, arrived at Store Hill.

The section ahead to Crawl indicated "Clear", so we continued to Aquarium Station, passing through Flatts Station and across the high level Flatts Bridge - with scenery that was always worth viewing: the old buildings of the Frascatti Hotel and scuba divers and sail boats in the translucent blue-green waters below.

Aquarium Station was packed with tourists returning to their cruise boat but Shelly Bay Station, our next port of call, was deserted - unlike the situation on horse racing days, when it was packed with fortune hunters, or on Saturday nights when the last eastbound train almost invariably collected a motley bunch of drunks

whose antics sometimes required the use of the fire
extinguishers and the threat of the crank handle to
restore order. I remember one night when the conductor
was missing on arrival at Crawl - physically thrown off
by a jolly rider in 2nd class! The train was backed up
to find the victim knocked out near the race track,
with his tickets and money strewn around; I believe
that it was this incident which led to the granting of
the powers of Special Constable to all train
conductors.

Aquarium Station - but not with crowds awaiting the Boat Train! Note, beyond
the station nameboard overlooking the highway, the signal telephone cabin.

Today, no such troubles! We clocked in at Crawl and
continued onwards to Bailey's Bay Station, via the long
Bailey's Bay Trestle below the high water datum, where
the scheduled down train came into the passing loop.

The down train obtained clearance to continue its
journey, but the Ferry Point instrument refused us
access and showed the "Red Flag", probably meaning that
the swing bridge over the waterway to Ferry Reach and
Harrington Sound was open.

Bailey's Bay Station with passengers disembarking, not from a Boat Train, but from an eastbound "Special". Note the horse-drawn taxis awaiting their fares. The loco headboard reads: "St. GEORGES. Aquarium, Bailey's Bay, Hamilton"

We waited whilst the complicated exercise of opening and, then, closing the bridge was completed - after which the flag at Bailey's Bay showed "Clear" and we were able to move off into the Ferry Point block section. Just a couple of passengers left us at Coney Island Station, then we were running across the long Coney Island Trestle - with breathtaking views in both directions (but especially to the right) - as we arrived at the swing bridge, with its black ball displayed at the mast head to indicate to shipping that the channel was closed. Ahead of us the bridge keeper appeared, red flag waving until he was happy that we had reduced our speed to just 5 mph, and then we enjoyed the hollow metallic rumble of wheels on steel until we reached dry land again below the Matello Tower on the tip of St George's Island.

On leaving Ferry Point Station and, adjacent to it, the site where the railway scrap yard had once been, we would next make our way along the straight stretch of track - passing the private halt used by passengers on Vincent Astor's private narrow gauge railway - towards Oil Docks Station. However, control advised me that there was a train shunting the railway's only tank car (filled with crude oil bound for the Elbow Beach Hotel's siding at Ord Road Station) at Oil Docks - and this was confirmed by the "Red Flag" showing, once more, in the token instrument and barring my withdrawing the key for the final block section to St George. I knew, sitting here waiting for clearance to proceed, that the driver of the oil tank train would have taken a key at Ferry Point, enabling him to unlock the siding switch at Oil Docks. The key would have become captive in the switch machine and the tank wagon would have been shunted down to the West India Oil Co filling station. By now I knew that the driver would have reset the switch for the main line and removed his key before inserting it in the Oil Docks Siding machine - clearing the block at Ferry Point. Sure enough, the relay tinkled, the flag went "White" and, on my taking a key, the flag changed to "Green" and portrayed the legend "Train Going to". The block section was now re-locked for our entry - and we were off.

The nice, straight downhill track ahead allowed me to make up a bit of time, for after all the delays were now running quite a few minutes late. I just hoped that one of Farmer Packwood's cows would not be in the middle of track, as it had been on occasions in the past, requiring the conductor to show his cowboy skills in clearing the way ahead. This had, to be fair, not occurred recently - not since a train driver had failed to see the wretched beast one evening at dusk and had turned the animal to beefburgers in the process of becoming derailed. Hopefully the court action against Mr Packwood would discourage him from blocking the line in the future!

We passed, the informally named, Ferry Reach Junction, with no sign of either of Astor's two locomotives, and Oil Docks Station, where we could see in the distance the oil tank wagon still coupled to the shunting loco. There was minimum passenger activity at either Mullet Bay or Wellington Stations, and soon we were rattling across the level crossings and complicated switch work as we arrived at St George Station - not too far behind schedule. As my train was a "Boat Train Special", the station staff had set the manual siding switch for the "dockside" siding and we drew to a halt within easy walking distance of the tourists' floating hotel - the *Prince David*.

Before considering the journey completely over, I still had some activity to undertake: report in at the signal cabin, and receive train orders for the return journey. Only immediately prior to departure, would a key would be taken out again - just in case another train wished to "get in", or more shunting on the main line was required at Oil Docks.

The nifty yard shunter uncoupled No 100, and I drove it around the train ready for the return journey - by which time I would have re-positioned the train at the "Town" Station Siding ready for the use of the regular passengers.

Another Bermuda railway journey had been safely completed!

THE FERRY REACH RAILWAY

The standard gauge Bermuda Railway did not hold exclusive running rights over all rails laid on the islands! The military authorities laid down a number of narrow gauge lines for the moving of stores and ammunition at various of the fortifications and at HM Dockyard; on Boaz Island, a railed slipway existed for carrying seaplanes from inside the Great Sound to outside - or vice versa - to obtain the best water conditions for flying off and recovery after landing. (The hangar and one section of slipway can still be seen today at Runway Lane, Boaz Island.) Additionally, of course, the ship and boat yards had rails laid on slipways for moving vessels to and from the water for routine maintenance and repair - and there existed a few garden layouts belonging to railway modelling enthusiasts. However, by far the most impressive other railway system in Bermuda was the Ferry Reach Railway.

Displaying a good head of steam, the replica Baltimore and Ohio Railroad 2-6-0 "Mainliner" runs through the Ferry Road Tunnel and into the gardens of Ferry Reach House. This picture was taken during Mr Herbert Biermann's ownership of the line.

Variously known as Ferry Reach Railway and Ferry Reach Railways, the line had been built in 1934 for the well known celebrity Vincent Astor, who had made his main home on St George's Island, by Harold Kitchen. Many a time these two pillars of commerce and society could be seen relaxing from the various stresses of live by "playing trains", wearing (of course!) the appropriate livery and engine driver caps.

The 24" gauge line ran from Astor's impressive Ferry Reach House residence, through a tunnel under Ferry Road, and north west across open shrubland to reach the Bermuda Railway main line at what was, unofficially, known as Ferry Reach Junction. Here a private halt was located for the main railway - together with the little railway's own running sheds. In the grounds of Ferry Reach House, a branch line ran through an attractive cutting to the swimmimg pool, jetty and summer house (part of which was used as a secondary engine shed).

The Running Sheds on the North Shore, with both the "Mainliner" and the "Utility" on parade, and with Mr William Kitchen at the controls of the 2-6-0. Note at that on this date (1951) the "Mainliner" carried the markings FERRY REACH and 999, but was not carrying the brass bell.

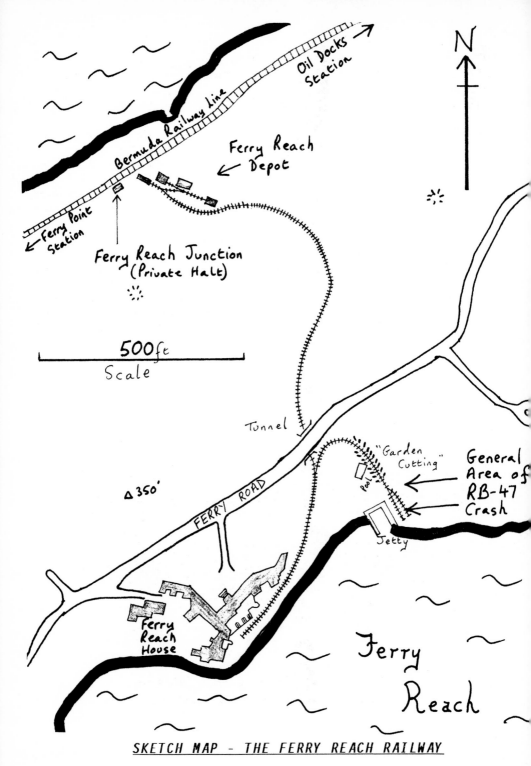

N

Oil Docks Station

Bermuda Railway Line

Ferry Reach Depot

Ferry Point Station

Ferry Reach Junction (Private Halt)

500ft
Scale

Tunnel

"Garden Cutting"

General Area of RB-47 Crash

Pool

Jetty

Δ 350'

FERRY ROAD

Ferry Reach House

Ferry Reach

SKETCH MAP - THE FERRY REACH RAILWAY

Painted black, with white running gear and funnel (smokestack), the major item of rolling stock was a minature version of the American Baltimore & Ohio Railroad's 2-6-0 "Mainliner" locomotive, which had been built for Astor by the B&O, of which company he was Chairman. The locomotive burnt oil rather than coal, but gave off an impressive plume of steam, and, in Astor's time, carried the number "999" on the cab door and the name "Ferry Reach" on the streamling above the driving wheels, together with a fine brass bell on top of the boiler. In addition to the "Mainliner", the railway possessed an battery powered "Utility" loco - a converted mining unit fitted out to carry three passengers, plus the driver - and a baggage car. The "Utility" carried no number but, at different times in its career, carried the words "Ferry Reach" on either both sides or on the end of the body. As one can well imagine, Vincent Astor took great pride in meeting his many important visitors at Ferry Reach Junction and conveying them home by his private railway.

A 1951 view of the "Utility", standing in the open countryside to the North of the Ferry Road Tunnel.

Minus cab, bell and streamlining, and eaten with rust, the replica "Mainliner" stands forlornly at the rear of Ferry Reach House.

Garden Cutting in 1992 - still with the lines *in situ* and the cutting walls in pristine condition.

The building of the Kindley Field Air Base, with the main take-off and landing paths of the aircraft being directly over Ferry Reach House, removed from Astor the peace and tranquility that he enjoyed in Bermuda and eventually he sold his estate to Lord and Lady Mitchell, who were not railway enthusiasts and allowed the system to fall into disrepair.

It was the presence of the air base which led to further disaster for the Ferry Reach and its railway, for in the early hours of the morning of 27th October 1962, during the Cuban Crisis, a RB-47 reconnaissance jet failed to gain height on take-off from Kindley and crashed on to the Ferry Reach summer house, killing all four aircrew on board.

In 1967 the estate was bought by Mr Herbert Biermann, who had visions of mining stone from the area. He set about recovery of the railway and had the "mainliner" restored to full running order, painted red with the cab top white, but with neither number nor name displayed. For four more years a plume of steam could once again be seen running between Ferry Reach Junction - now a junction no more, of course - and the main house, but Biermann's plans to cut vast quantities of stone from the headland were quashed by the Government and he died a broken man in 1971 - the last year in which trains ran over these metals.

Today the rails are still *in situ* and in good condition, although very overgrown in places, and most of the buildings on the north shore still stand - albeit in a very weather beaten state. Sadly, an attempt by the Railway Museum to aquire the "Mainliner" failed and it now stands, as a silent tribute to Bermuda's second railway, in decay to the rear of Ferry Reach House and probably beyond realistic restoration. I can find no details of the final disposal of the "Utility" loco; my last record is of it being seen, in very bad condition, at the Ferry Reach Depot, on the North Shore, in 1988.

THE LINE TODAY

An island as beautiful as Bermuda cries out to be explored; there is no finer way to do this than to travel, in your own time, along the the right of way which once carried the Bermuda Railway.

NOTE: Eighteen of the twenty two miles of trackbed that once crossed the Island of Bermuda were designated in 1985 as *Railway Trail*, and are well sign-posted; additionally, a pamphlet describing the trail - from a non-railway point of view - can be obtained from any of the Island's three Tourist Information Centres (in Hamilton, St George and Somerset).

The sections of trail from Somerset Bus Station to Somerset Bridge, from Paynter Lane or Store Lane to Tribe Road No 5 (Southampton) and from Cedar Hurst Place (Evans Bay Station) to Middle Road at Frank's Bay are tarmac surfaced and ideal for exploration from moped as well as from horseback, pedal cycle or by foot.

With the exception of short sections of the trackbed that have been converted to public highway, the rest of the signposted trail is not truly suitable for moped travel - and in some places signs proclaiming "No Motor Vehicles" will be found, together with locked gates and low level stiles.

In the vicinity of Hamilton, the section from Trimingham Hill, along Front Street and out to the North East and Palmetto Road is not designated as *Railway Trail*; it can be even be explored by car!

JOURNEY ONE - SOMERSET to HAMILTON

Today, as in years gone by, the journey from Somerset to Hamilton commences at Somerset Station (now a bus and not a railway station), which lies off Beacon Hill Road, adjacent to the Police Station. As is immediately obvious, the pink painted building is the old railway terminus, the line in its active years continuing just beyond here into the the grass area furthest from the roadway. As you follow the *Railway Trail* signs away from Beacon Hill Road, you pass the sites of Broome Street and Scotts Hill Stations - located at the points where the trail crosses the roads of these same names. Note on your right, after leaving Bob's Valley Road, the section of rail still standing at the side of the

<u>Somerset Station - now in use as a bus terminus.</u>

trail: this marks the site of Sound View Station, and
is shortly followed by a new bridge over Sound View
Drive - where the wooden Harman's Bay Trestle once
stood, and from whence you can experience the views
that yesteryear's rail travellers once enjoyed. If you
wish to appreciate the elevated nature of the line,
backtrack for just a short distance, turn left along
Sound View Road until Sound View Drive and go down the
drive to the base of the modern bridge and look up at
the bridge railings above. Although concrete has
replaced wood, the bridge dimensions are not dissimilar
to those of its predecessor.

Back on the *Railway Trail*, and just before reaching the
outer defence works of Fort Scaur, note the tall,
rusting section of rail set back into the rock face of
the cutting; this is one of the few remaining poles
that carried the communication wires of the signalling
system, though it is not a signal post in the normally
accepted sense. Parapet Trestle once straddled the
marked dip in the ground, and the trail, that you
shortly encounter.

After crossing Lantana Road, you will enter the
beautiful cutting of the same name, with its two
attractive wooden accommodation bridges far overhead,
and then travel along an attractive, low embankment to
Somerset Bridge Station - now in use by a business
trading as "Simons Upholstery". This was the first
passing loop out of the terminus, indicated by the
width of the *Railway Trail* at this point.

Somerset Bridge Station - now trading as "Simons Upholstery".

As the trail eases to the right, note ahead of you the
concrete footings for the landward sections of the
Somerset Railway Bridge; if you are walking, proceed
alongside them but, if riding, continue to join Middle
Road and shortly afterwards turn left along Wharf
Drive. From here you have an excellent view of the
plinths which carried the high level bridge across the
waterway joining together Great Sound and Ely's
Harbour.

Regaining the public highway, cross the diminutive
Somerset (Road) Bridge and then rejoin the *Railway*

Trail by turning into Paynter Lane. Before turning right at the end, travel the short distance back to the water's edge and appreciate the site of the dismantled bridge from the opposite direction. Here, where the upright section of rail still stands, stood Bridge Hill Station. As you follow the trail along the perimeter fence of the United States Navy Annex - itself, at the time of writing, soon to become part of Bermuda's history - you will pass White Hill Station, which is now in use as a manufacturing unit for furniture components, and then the site of George's Bay Road Station, which stood next to the present US Base entrance. Note, as you continue southwards, another section of vertically mounted rail on the left hand side of the trail: no timetabled station stood here; it was the site of a Privilege Halt.

Evan's Bay Station, now in use as a Sunday School. *The Railway Trail* crosses the main road here and continues to the left of the bus shelter on the right of the photograph.

As you cross Tribe Road No 5, the paved surface gives way to a grassy path down to rejoin Middle Road. It was

here that Evan's Pond Trestle carried the line over the
highway and then through a shallow cutting to Evan's
Bay Station. If you are walking, cross the road and
climb the rough steps to rejoin the trail as it runs
alongside Port Royal Golf Course, noting as you do so
the massive bridge abutment still in place at the
roadside.

Eight of the eleven concrete plinths which carried the
line above the foreshore at Frank's Bay. In the distance can
be seen some of the scattered islands of The Great Sound.

Today Evan's Bay Station is in use as the Sunday School
for Emmanuel Methodist Church; follow the easily
engineered section from here to Frank's Bay where, from
Middle Road, you can view the 11 concrete plinths which
mark the former site of the trestle that carried the
line across this stretch of water to Frank's Bay
Station. Although not accessible to the public, the
routing of the railway is still readily apparent on
your left hand side until just after the junction of
Middle and South Shore Roads.

On entering this "no motor vehicles" section note, prior to the gate, the Public Works department marker in the grass at the mouth of the deep, dramatic cutting - which ends, with a single remaining section of railway-associated concrete underfoot, where the residents of Newport Gardens now reside. Here stood Church Road Trestle, and its southern abutment is clearly visible where Church Road meets Middle Road, next to Southampton Post Office. Before climbing the steps to regain the former trackbed, note the old stonework incorporated into the PO lawn.

The remains of Church Road Station's platforms can be picked out on both sides of the old permanent way - then take note of the set of steps on your left, which gave access to the station from the road and foreshore below (and still bears traces of the original paintwork).

The entrance to the impressive cutting taking the trackbed away from Middle Road to follow the contours below Gibb's Hill and its famous cast iron lighthouse.

Another impressive cutting now lies ahead, swinging to the right to follow the contours around the ridge upon which Gibbs Hill Lighthouse stands. After crossing the steep Tribe Road which lies ahead, abeam Black Bay - and where the sidings of that name were located - note the discarded section of rail, with chair still attached, which failed to make the journey south to British Guiana! The marked dip in the trail, which now lies ahead of you as you leave the stone cutting directly below the lighthouse, marks the location of the Mallory Trestle - of which no traces of the structure now remain.

As you cross Lighthouse Road and enter the section of the *Railway Trail* renamed as Shawn Access Lane, note the remains of the Lighthouse Station platform on your left hand side. Then, as the new lane turns off the trail to the right, you come to the site of Lighthouse Trestle - where the railway was carried across the shallow ravine at the head of which the Southampton Princess Hotel now dominates the southern skyline. Steps lead down to permit you to cross and rejoin the elevated railbed next to a ruined building (which has no apparent railway connection).

Riddell's Bay Station building, looking towards Hamilton - with
The *Railway Trail* continuing through the cool, lush vegetation ahead.

Next, enjoy the meandering beauty of the old permanent
way until, after crossing Camp Hill Road, you come to
Riddell's Bay Station. No remains are apparent of the
trestle bearing this name, but one of the station
buildings still stands - the other having been replaced
by an electricity sub-station. The deep sandy dip that
you soon encounter as you come off an easy right hand
curve in the trackbed marks the location of Sharp's
Trestle - and it was here that I came across a chair
spike in the summer of 1992 (almost 45 years after it
must have been dropped during salvaging operations).

"The meandering beauty of the old permanent way".

From here the track suffers from the encroachment of
modern housing but, between the built up areas. it is
still possible to blot the present from one's mind and
to anticipate the arrival of a train from Hamilton
around one of the many gentle curves in the track!

The steep drop in the trail into the Quarry Lane
Industrial Site marks the location of Warwick Pond
Trestle and of Kyber Pass Station. Then (continuing

eastwards) note, after crossing Warwick Tribe Road No 3
and passing through a shallow cutting topped with lush
vegetation, the next marked dip in the *Railway Trail* -
which is where Morgan's Trestle once stood.

As you cross Ord Road for the first time, you will note
ahead of you the bus parking bay: this is where, when
buses were still only a future possibility, the trains
stopped to drop off and collect passengers at the
Belmont Manor Station. From here the former trackbed
runs alongside the golf course, until the surface turns
to a paved one and you reach the junction of the trail
and Cobb's Hill Road. On your right hand side before
the road, note the last remaining vestiges of the
Cobb's Hill Station's platform.

The next section of the trail is truly rural - very
quiet and rarely overlooked - until you come for a
second time to Ord Road. The platform remains can just
be picked out at the edge of the private garden on your
right; the slight widening of the track on the left
marks the short siding where the Elbow Beach Hotel tank
wagon - water, then oil - was parked in former years.

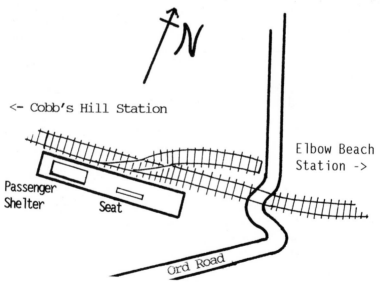

Sketch showing the layout at Ord Road Station in operating days. The siding (on
your left as you approach Ord Road) was used to stable the 5,000 gallon oil wagon,
from which fuel was drawn for the Elbow Beach Hotel's heating system. In earlier
years water for the hotel had been pumped from this siding to the hotel.

Another quiet stretch of trackbed brings you across the busy South Road and to the site of Elbow Beach Station - where the building still stands and currently houses the Headquarters of "The Bermuda Junior Chamber".

The Elbow Beach station building. Once an alighting point for the South Shore beaches, it now houses the Headquarters of the Bermuda Junior Chamber of Commerce.

Continuing towards Hamilton, an attractive embankment carries the old line past Paget Marsh, and past the former location of Rural Hill Station on Grape Bay Drive; then, as the embankment gives way to a cutting, the Ardsheal Drive overbridge draws your eye nicely towards the 450′ long Rural Hill (or Paget) Tunnel, which allowed the line to pass below South Road and on towards Trimingham Hill. The station serving the hospital stood adjacent to the "Hospital" sign on your right hand side.

The *Railway Trail* ends as you cross the entrance to Trimingham Drive; the railway itself followed the side of the present Trimingham Road, until the impressive Springfield Trestle carried it across the end of

Hamilton Harbour as far as where Crow Lane Bakery now stands. Save for one piece of stonework near the Foot of the Lane Roundabout, no traces of the trestle remain today.

The Northern Portal of Rural Hill Tunnel. Here The *Railway Trail* crosses below busy South Road.

The old locomotive depot site is lost beneath the new four lane highway leading towards Front Street, whilst the site of Middle Road Station - at the present junction of Lane Hill and Crow Lane - also reveals no traces of its former existence. The old corrugated iron building housing a motorcycle business on your right hand side, just after Lane Hill is of interest - it marks the point where the yard exit to Hamilton was located, and was built originally as a NAAFI canteen to serve British service personnel.

Finally, as did the railway run of old, our journey in from Somerset ends opposite the Cenotaph on Front Street. Although it is easy to imagine the "Rattle & Shake" traversing most of the path that we have travelled, busy Front Street today shows no real trace of its railway heritage.

JOURNEY TWO - ST GEORGE to HAMILTON

The station building of the St George Terminus still
stands on the edge of Tiger Bay Gardens, located in
Wellington Street adjacent to McCallan's Wharf. Note
the distinctive slope at the western end of the old
platform - the only one on the island - and the two
vertically embedded sections of rail on the exterior
wall of what is now the premises of "St George Signs".

The former station building at St George Terminus, with a modern
cruise liner alongside McCallan's Wharf. The road running behind
the old building is Wellington Street, leading to the town centre.

The former trackbed can easily be traced to the left of
the highway as far as Wellington Park, the Wellington
Station having once been sighted here.

Today's Wellington Lane follows the railway lineation
then, shortly after the paved surface gives way to

- 69 -

sandy soil, the site of the Mullet Bay Trestle lies
ahead of you - concrete plinths, rusted iron fittings
and embedded timbers indicating its location. Here, on
the edge of the modern Rock Hill Park, stood Mullet Bay
Station.

Beautiful walking countryside - in this case the old trackbed to West of Oil
Docks Station. In the far distance can be seen buildings of the naval dockyard.

Note, as you follow the trail alongside the shore
enjoying the views experienced by the passengers of
old, the signalling system pole quietly rusting away in
the next cutting. After a quarter of a mile, you come
to a further rusting pole and then the Shell Oil
Refinery security fence. Retrace your steps and drop
back down onto Ferry Road until clear of the Shell
installation, when you can rejoin the *Railway Trail*
near the Shell Gas Depot. (On this detour from the old
permanent way, you will have missed the locations of
Oil Dock Station and the Gulley and Oil Docks
Trestles.)

After a section of the line giving dramatic distant
views across the water to the Dockyard, you come - now
two miles from St George - to the four buildings at
Ferry Reach Junction: the end of Vincent Astor's 24"

gauge line from his house on Ferry Reach's north shore.
All but one of the buildings have succumbed to the
ravages of time and weather - that with no roof or
walls being a victim of Hurricane Emily - but you can
still see unlifted sections of track and pointwork.

The *Railway Trail* now continues, past the site of Ferry
Point Station (located where the trail and Ferry Road
meet), to the northern end of Ferry Point Bridge, which
once crossed the waterway in from unrestricted ocean to
Ferry Reach and, then, St George's Harbour. Note, as
you look at the concrete plinths and cross members
still standing proudly clear of the water, the
variation in general shape of the remains: this is
where the swing element of the bridge was located.

From here it is necessary to return via The Causeway to
reach Coney Island; however, don't backtrack along the
line, but follow Ferry Road back towards the Oil Depot.
Note, as you travel down the road with a long section
of chain link fence on your right hand side, the short
tunnel carrying the Ferry Reach Railway track below the
highway and, in the grounds of Ferry Reach House, the
attractive little cutting in the garden and more of the
remaining narrow gauge rails. Finally, on this stretch
of highway, as you approach the "Y" junction ahead, you
are passing the point where the proposed extension to
Kindley Field would have crossed over Ferry Road.

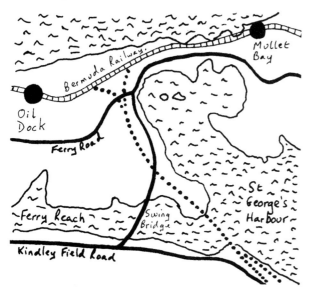

Proposed Military Extension
to Kindley Field (........)

It was never built.

A good view of the remaining artefacts of the Ferry
Point and Coney Island bridges can be seen as you go
across The Causeway; leave the main road after passing
the Perfume Factory and make your way along Coney
Island Road to its end by the Government Fisheries
establishment.

Ferry Point Bridge, looking from the Northern tip of Coney
Island towards St George's Island. Note the point in the middle
of the waterway where the swing element of the bridge was located.

From this, the southern end of Ferry Point Bridge, the
trackbed crosses Coney Island Park in a cutting with
only one substantial wall and, adjacent to the road and
where 9 single and 2 double plinths of the Coney Island
Bridge remain on both land and in the sea, traverses
what is now the Bailey's Bay Cricket Club ground.
Continuing across Duck's Puddle Drive - past the site
of Coney Island Station - the trail runs along the
water's edge until the obvious locations of Henry's
Hill Bridge (note the discarded length of rail on the
rocks below) and Outerbridge's Trestle are reached.
Shortly thereafter, note the site of Bailey's Bay
Station - where the tall wall stands on your left, next
to the bus stop and parallel highway.

On reaching beautiful Bailey's Bay, look ahead at the 6 large and 3 small plinths which once supported the Bailey's Bay Trestle over the water as the line continued along its route to Hamilton.

On rejoining *The Railway Trail*, after skirting the bay on the public North Shore Road, you will be on arguably one of the most enchanting stretches of coastal railway trackbed in the world, let alone in Bermuda! After the site of the private (and non-timetabled) Bailey's Bay Halt, pass the Clay's Bay and Sisson's Trestles sites in quick succession until, through a major cutting and on a falling gradient, you reach the site of Crawl Station. Today, only the remains of the building base act as a reminder of its passing. Note ahead of you, as you leave Crawl and turn left onto Crawl Hill to rejoin North Shore Road for a short while, the remaining low plinths of the Crawl Trestle.

The sole remaining artefacts of the Clay's Bay Trestle. Although almost all of the structure has long disappeared, note the last vestiges of ironwork - left behind after the cutting torches had done their work in 1948.

Turn off the highway into Old Road. Call in at Burchall
Cove to view the narrow sea passage into the cove, over
which the railway passed on the Burchall Cove Bridge,
before continuing along Old Road until the *Railway
Trail* sign - the site of Shelley Bay Station, which
served the old racecourse as well as the resort - where
you must double back on yourself to view the remains of
Five Mile Trestle.

On arrival at Shelley Bay itself, look for the
embankment behind the beach where the trackbed lay and
where, still, the few remains of the Shelley Bay
Trestle nestle beneath the tamarisk bushes.

Aquarium Station - with this building housing the Bermuda Railway
Museum. The chairs in the foreground are important relics in their
own right, having been used in 1st class accommodation on the railway!

After another short excursion off the trail, rejoin the
track on a lightly engineered section until you arrive
at Aquarium Station. Here you will find still standing
the old station building and freight shed - housing the
truly excellent Bermuda Railway Museum (open Tuesday to
Saturday 10am to 4pm, and Sundays 12 noon to 4pm) - and
a signal telephone shelter. Stop awhile to visit and

admire the Museum, only opened in February 1992 but
already the island's centre for Bermuda Railway Company
artefacts, photographs and railway memorabilia.

The land beyond the Museum (containing the remains of
the base of the trestle approach to Flatts Bridge) is
in private ownership, and leads down to the remains of
Flatts Bridge itself - built across the entrance to
Flatts Inlet and Harrington Sound, and through which
tremendous tidal races surge as they did, of course, in
railway years.

The main concrete plinths of the 40' high Flatt's Bridge, completely different in
shape of those at the other high bridge - Somerset Bridge. Across the fast-flowing
water stands the trackbed leading to Aquarium Station; behind, stand the remains
of Flatts West Trestle and the steps up from North Shore Road to Flatts station.

Make your way around the inlet, through Flatts village,
until you reach the prominent abutment of the Flatts
West Trestle; opposite there, walk down to the water's
edge by the public park to admire the extensive remains
of the Flatts Bridge foundations - noting as you go,

and before the access path slopes downwards, the two iron securing bolts still standing proud of the ground, with one even bearing traces of its original coat of paint!

Crossing the main road to its other side, climb the steps which led up to Flatts Station and follow the trackbed westwards, passing under the bridge to Magnolia Hall and on through one of Bermuda's most dramatic railway cuttings, until reaching the 4 pillars which supported the Store Hill Trestle, and within which sections of cut-off girder and fixings are still readily apparent. Cross Store Hill roadway itself and the site of Store Hill Station lies one hundred yards or so to the westwards on the edge of Penhurst Park.

On leaving the area of the park, cross Cable Hill - the site of both Gibbon's and Cox's Trestles - and look out for the stonework of the latter, still clearly visible on the seaward side of the track. Finally, on this rural stretch of the old line, come to the remains of Devonshire Trestle - with its "Danger Bridge Removed" sign (the only such sign on the whole of the old line) erected near to the site of Devonshire Station. The western section of the formal element of The *Railway Trail* ends just after here, as you pass the earthworks of Fort Langton and enter Palmetto Road.

To follow the old orientation of the line towards the city, continue along Palmetto Road in a south-westerly direction, the line being either on, or adjacent to, the left hand side of the highway. Prospect Station stood at the present confluence of Dock Hill and the aptly named Junction Lane, adjacent to which you will note the equally aptly named Trackside Lane. The next indication of a railway connection comes up as you reach Railway Terrace - so named because the line ran along here before the housing stock was built up - and the site of the former Pond Hill Station (where the line crossed what is now called Border Lane North and South).

Race Course Station stood where the gateway now is to the Refuse Disposal Plant, with the private halt serving Government House standing where, today, the edge of Paget Marsh abuts Marsh Folly Road.

Drop down off this wide road onto Canal Road and, although the station remains have long gone, the buildings of the Tennis Club indicate where Tennis Stadium Station was located. Only yards beyond here, look up and admire from both sides the attractive Laffan Street overbridge.

The deep cutting running past the tennis stadium. The Laffan Street Bridge can be seen beyond the two concrete braces.

Until it meets Brooklyn Lane, Canal Road (named after a drainage, rather than a navigation, canal) marks the line of the old railway; beyond here it follows Serpentine Road, which had a station of that name standing at the present junction of Serpentine and Woodlands Roads.

The station serving the Bermudiana Hotel - also known as Richmond Road Station, (originally intended as a passing loop only) - was located where the Esso Automart garage now stands, but from here until Front Street road re-alignment (Par-La-Ville Road is a "new"

road) and major alterations to the buildings make it
impossible to follow the old railway route exactly. The
Richmond Tunnel, which allowed the track to pass below
the Par-La-Ville Gardens before regaining the light of
day to the West of the famous Police Birdcage has been
eliminated, so follow the one way Par-La-Ville Road
down to Pitts Bay Road; the southern tunnel portal
stood where you now see the Harold Haye Frith Building
on your left hand side.

Pitt's Bay Road. Believe it or not, this was where the Richmond Road
Tunnel below Par-La-Ville Gardens once stood! The entrance to Somers
Building (the taller building) stood next to the right hand side of
the tunnel mouth, the left hand side being positioned roughly where
the word "free" appears in the window of the shop called Bananas.

To conclude your journey following the old route from
St George to Hamilton, it is only necessary to proceed
along Front Street, passing No 1 Shed - beside which
was located Queen Street Station - to reach The
Cenotaph and the site of Parliament Street Terminal.
"Tickets, please!"

ROLLING STOCK

A general view of the East Broadway Yard (*circa* 1933), shortly after a delivery of loco fuel. In the foreground, from left to right, stand a 1st Class Chair Car, Locomotive No 101 and a "Toast Rack". Note, in the distance beyond the Key Token Hut, the Planet Shunter.

The original rolling stock for the railway was built at the Preston, Lancashire works of the English Electric Co for the Drewry Car Company Ltd, England, for delivery by 1931 and consisted of:

Six 120 hp, 20 ton petrol-engined composite 1st & 2nd class passenger cars - numbered 10 to 15, inclusive. Seating capacity was for 16 1st class and 26 2nd class passengers. (For greater detail of these units, see Annex 1.)

Two 120 hp, 35′ long, 20 ton petrol-engined motorised freight vans - numbered 30 and 31. (See Annex 2.)

Six 14 ton 1st class passenger coaches - 42′ in length and numbered 20 to 25, inclusive (known as "Pullmans").

Two 14 ton trailer freight vans (box cars), numbers 40 and 41.

Additionally, some rolling stock - including a 60 hp "Planet" contractors locomotive and a motorised inspection speeder - was retained in Bermuda after the completion of construction work, together with a small amount of ex-Russian freight stock. A 5,000 gallon oil tank wagon was also purchased by the railway at some unspecified, but early, date. Two 10 ton capacity flat cars, bearing the numbers 70 and 71 were used by the railway - the latter possibly being the rebuild of motor coach 12 after it was gutted by fire (see Annex 1).

In 1932 the following rolling stock was added to the fleet:

Two petrol-engined motorised freight vans - renumbered 100 (*Towne of St George*) and 101 (*City of Hamilton*), after initially being numbered 60 and 61. (For greater detail of these units, see Annex 3.)

Four "Gondola" cars (open, drop-sided, bogie goods wagons) - numbered 50 to 53, inclusive.

Six 2nd class "Toast Rack" passenger coaches - numbered 60 to 65, inclusive.

In 1942 and 1943 the following additions, imported from the USA, were added to the fleet:

Two 300 hp diesel-electric locomotives, which bore the numbers 200 and 201. (For greater detail of these units, see Annex 4.)

All locomotives were speed-governed to a maximum of 30 mph and, in view of the proximity of trains and pedestrians and livestock, fitted with USA-style "cowcatchers".

An additional passenger coach bearing the number 26 was built from "parts" in the Company shops in 1937.

The original colour scheme for the rolling stock was of primrose yellow bodywork, with brown striping, and with brown lettering outlined in green. The bogies and underside areas were painted black, whilst the side rods, counterweights and draw beams carried red paint. To reflect the heat, the roofs were painted white.

In 1936 the distinctive primrose livery gave way to one of maroon (similar to that of the London, Midland & Scottish Railway in Great Britain), with yellow lettering and striping. The underbody areas remained painted black and the roofs retained their white colour scheme. Locos No 200 and 201 were finished off in natural metal colouring.

Classic Bermuda Scene: one of the composite motor coaches, in the original colour scheme, stands at Hamilton, with the Cenotaph just visible to the right amongst the palm trees. The background scenery remains virtually unchanged today.

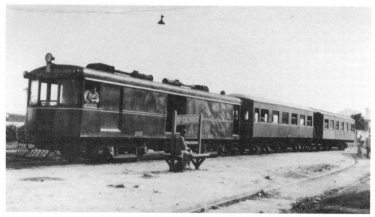

No 200 stands at the entrance to St George Station with a two coach train. Behind the loco can be seen the waters of St George's Harbour and, beyond, military buildings on St David's Island.

The ex-Balfour Beatty 60 hp "Planet" loco, used extensively for shunting duties. It was fitted with a 4 cylinder Bagule petrol engine, a 4 speed reversable "crash change" gear box - but no electric starter!

Seen at the Oil Dock Wharf, this 5,000 gallon oil tank wagon was used to carry fuel to the siding at Ord Road Station.

Rolling stock in the yard in 1947. Motorised freight van No 30, stands on the left; its cannibalised contemporary No 30 stands on the right, behind two "Gondolas" - the nearer of which is No 53, and the further that converted to a fuel wagon. By now the yard was being shared by the vehicles operating the Hamilton to Somerset bus service.

In another sad view towards the end of operations in Bermuda, No 31 stands forlornly behind the "Planet" loco. Note, through the grime, the later years "BR1" marking on the shunter, together with the original markings lower down.

OUTLINE TECHNICAL DATA:
MOTOR COACHES 10 to 15

Manufacturer	The English Electric Co, on behalf of the Drewry Car Co. The bodies were built by Cravens Ltd.
Eng. Elect Serial Nos:	832 to 837.
Number of Trucks	One motor; one trailer.
Service Weight	20 tons.
Truck Centres	25 feet.
Wheelbases	Motor truck: 6'6"; trailer truck: 5'6".
Length over Headstocks	42'0".
Width over Pillars	9'0".
Number of Driving Axles	Two: one driven by transmission; one driven by side rods, these being retro-fitted after delivery.

Two of the first series motor coaches, with No 15 on the right, utilising the passing loop at Store Hill Station.
(Driver Card and Conductor Prentice pose for the camera.)

Powerplant	Parsons Marine 6 cylinder, petrol (gasoline) engine, with magneto ignition, electric starting and dual Amal up draft carburettors. Centrifugally governed to 1,560 rpm.
Nominal Power	120 hp.
Fuel System	Originally fitted with 2 Tecalamet electric pumps; later changed to "Autopulse" system.
Transmission	Spicer shafts, driving a Wilson 5-speed preselective epicycle gearbox (fitted with integral reverse box), driving the powered axle via a 2'6" Morse chain. The gearbox controls were later modified by Wm Kitchen to single handle control, using the facilities of the Bermuda Workshops.
Control Stations	Stations at both ends of motor coaches. Normally operated as a motor trailer; could be operated as motor-trailer-motor combination.
Brakes	Continous pneumatic system, made by The Westinghouse Brake and Saxby Signal Co of Great Britain.
Air Compressors	Two twin-cylinder Westinghouse compressors, fitted with cylinder unloaders operating at 80 to 100 psi.
Electrical System	Two chain-driven Simms 3-brush generators, rated at 20 amps.
Lighting System	24 volt lead acid batteries in motor coach and trailer.

Cooling System   Water-cooled, with radiators
                                  at either end (upright at
                                  motor end; underslung at
                                  observation platform end).

Couplings   ABC semi-automatic, with no
                                  buffer requirement.

Additional data - Motor Coaches 10 to 15:

1.   No 12 was severly damaged by fire in 1943 and
     converted to a flat truck, possibly No 71.

2.   By 1945 all units had each operated over 25,000
     miles.

3.   Second class seating reduced from initial fit of
     26 seats to one of 24 seats.

OUTLINE TECHNICAL DATA:
MOTORISED FREIGHT VANS 30 and 31

Manufacturer	The English Electric Co, on behalf of the Drewry Car Co. Bodies built by Cravens Ltd.
Eng Elect Serial Nos	844 and 845.
Number of Trucks	One motor; one trailer.
Service Weight	20 tons.
Freight Capacity	10 tons.
Truck Centres	19'0".
Wheelbases	Motor truck: 6'6"; trailer truck: 5'6".
Length over Headstocks	35'0".

Additional data - Motorised Freight Vans 30 and 31:

1. Power plant, etc as in motor coaches 10 to 15.

2. Two doors each side for freight loading.

3. No 31 was taken out of service in 1944 to provide spares to keep the "Series 10" cars operating.

4. These units normally operated with trailer freight vans 40 and 41.

Photographs of the "30 Series" locos are not common. However, here we see No 31 on the dockside at St George, with a boat train serving the *SS Prince Henry*.

OUTLINE TECHNICAL DATA:
MOTOR LOCOS/FREIGHT VANS 100 and 101

Manufacturer	The English Electric Co, on behalf of the Drewry Car Co.
Eng Elect Serial Nos	867 and 868.
In Service Names	100: *City of Hamilton* 101: *Towne of St George*
Number of Motor Trucks	Two
Service Weight	29 tons.
Baggage Capacity	5 tons, split between 2 compartments at either end.
Truck Centres	19'6"
Wheelbase	7'0"
Number of Driving Axles	Four: One axle of each motor truck chain driven and the other side rod-coupled .
Nominal Power	300 hp (2 x 150 hp).

No 101, *Towne of St George*, stands outside the East Broadway running shed. Note, also, No 15 inside the shed undergoing maintenance.

Brakes	Westinghouse fully automatic, continous airbrake system.
Powerplants	Two Parsons Marine 8 cylinder, petrol (gasoline) engines, with Bosch-Simms magneto ignition, and dual Amal down draft carburettors. Centrifugally governed to 1,560 rpm.
Fuel System	Pressurised fuel tank (from airbrake system) reduced to 2 psi, with gravity-fed 1 imperial gallon header tank for each motor.
Transmission	Wilson Gearbox, with Drewry Car/Wackley Electro Pneumatic Control, driving the powered axles via 2'8" Morse chains.
Air Compressors	Four twin-cylinder Westinghouse compressors, fitted with mechanical unloaders operating at 80 to 100 psi and feeding an auxilary reservoir at controlled pressure of 70 psi.

No 101, carrying a "Special" headboard, with
a train of coral for use in track ballasting.

Electrical System	Two Bosch-Simms generators, driven by Reynolds chains from the associated engine card shaft.
Lighting System	24 volt lead acid batteries.
Cooling System	Two independent, water-cooled circuits, with vertical radiators at either end, fitted with a pump on each engine and supplemented by engine-driven fans.
Couplings	ABC semi-automatic, with no buffer requirement.

Additional data - Motor Locos/Freight Vans 100 and 101:

1. Designed to tow a minimum of 3 "Toast Rack" coaches.

2. Handled all the work in connection with the building of the American miitary bases.

OUTLINE TECHNICAL DATA:
DIESEL-ELECTRIC LOCOMOTIVES 200 and 201

Manufacturer	Cummins rebuilds of Brill Model 55 cars.
Number of Motors	Four.
Truck Centres	Approx 22'.
Number of Driving Axles	Four
Nominal Power	300 hp.

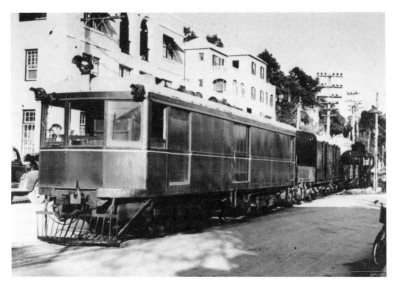

Locomotive No 200 with a goods train by Middle Road Station, with the 5,000 gallon oil tank wagon now carrying the name "Esso Fuel", instead of the earlier "West India Oil Co.". (This site is easily recognisable today; the nearest building being Hamma Galleries.)

Powerplant	Two Cummins Type "L", 6 cylinder, diesel-electric engines governed at 1,000 rpm and fitted with fuel injectors.

Fuel System	Cummins distributor system pump fitted.
Cooling System	Centrifugal circulating water pump fitted, with flow of 41 gallons per minute.
Couplings	ABC semi-automatic, with no buffer requirement.

Additional data - Diesel-Electric locos 200 and 201:

1. In the late 1930s The Cummins Engine Company, of Columbus Indiana, bought a number of Brill G-M cars for conversion to D-E for resale. In the same decade, a number of US railroad companies retired Brill cars that they were operating, particularly the popular Model 55s (43'6" long; 22'2" truck centres), and also the less used Model 65s (44'6" long; 22'3" truck centres).

2. The US Army bought units such as these in 1935 and it is believed that the finance to purchase 200 and 201 was provided by the US Army - probably from the Corps of Engineers budget - at $45,000 per unit.

3. No 200 was delivered to Bermuda in 1942; 201 arrived in 1943.

ADDITIONAL DATA - COACHES AND FREIGHT VANS:

1.   a.   The "Toast Rack" passenger coaches 60 to 65 were built as English Electric serial numbers 860 to 865. Seating capacity was for 68 passengers.

b.   Fitted with central entrance and exit doors, they were primarily purchased for the tourist and sightseeing traffic.

2.   a.   The "Pullman" passenger coaches 20 to 25 were built as English Electric serial numbers 838 to 843. Original seating capacity was for 40 in wicker armchairs, but this was later changed to 50/52 seats.

b.   Number 20 was removed from the Company's records by 1945, by which time all of this class had run for over 25,000 miles.

c.   No driving controls fitted; the dimensions were generally similar to motor coaches 10 to 15, except:

      i.   Weight: 14 tons.

      ii.   Wheelbase of both trucks: 5'6".

3.   a.   Two of the "Gondola" cars/wagons (50 & 51) had 15 ton capacity; 52 & 53 had 10 ton capacity.

b.   English Electric serial numbers 869 and 870 could possibly refer to 50 and 51.

c.   One of the larger cars, probably 51, was converted to a fuel tank wagon: 2,500 US gallons of petrol(gasoline) and 1,000 US gallons diesel.

4.   a.   Trailer freight vans 40 and 41 were of identical external dimensions to 30 and 31; however, in service weight was only 14 tons.

b.   English Electric serial numbers were 846 and 847.

c.   Normally pulled by motorised freight vans 30 and 31.

BERMUDA RAILWAY STATIONS/HALTS

Station	Serving	Status Today
*#Somerset	Somerset Town and tourist attractions. Nearest station to Naval Dockyard	In use as bus depot

The "end of the line": Somerset Station, in 1933, with No 15 - Conductor
Stanley Acton - ready to depart with a service to Hamilton

Broom Street	Somerset Suburbs	No obvious signs
Scott's Hill	Somerset Suburbs	No obvious signs
Sound View	Somerset Suburbs	One upright rail section
*#Somerset Bridge	Somerset Wharf and Ely's Harbour	In use as "Simon's Upholstery"
Bridge Hill	Rural Area	No obvious signs
*#White Hill	Rural Area	In use for furniture manufacturing
George's Bay Rd	Rural Area	No obvious signs
*#Evan's Bay	Agricultural Centre	Sunday School
Frank's Bay	Somers Boys College	No obvious signs
Church Road	Church Bay Beach	Steps and platform edge
Lighthouse	Gibb's Hill Lighthouse	Traces of platform
*#Riddell's Bay	Warwick Camp and Ridell's Bay Golf Course	Station Building

Kyber Pass	Rural Area	No obvious signs
Belmont	Belmont Manor Estate and Golf Course	No obvious signs
#Cobb's Hill	South Shore Beaches	Traces of platform
Ord Road	Elbow Beach Hotel Siding and South Shore Beaches	Traces of platform
*Elbow Beach	Elbow Beach Hotel and South Shore Beaches	Junior Chamber of Commerce Room
Rural Hill	Rural Area	Tunnel
Hospital	King Edward VII Hospital	No obvious signs
Middle Road	Hamilton Suburbs	No obvious signs
Hamilton (Cenotaph)	City Centre and Government Buildings	No obvious signs
Queen Street	No 1 Shed and major stores	No obvious signs
*#Richmond Road	Bermudiana Hotel	No obvious signs
Serpentine Road	Hamilton Suburbs	No obvious signs
Tennis Stadium	Tennis Club	No obvious signs
Government House	Private Halt	No obvious signs
Pond Hill	Hamilton Outer Suburbs	No obvious signs
Prospect	Kitchener Barracks	No obvious signs
Devonshire	Golf and Country Club	No obvious signs
*#Store Hill	Wireless Station	No obvious signs
Flatts	Flatts Village, Frascati Hotel and Golf Course	Access steps to platform level
*#Aquarium	Government Aquarium	In use as The Railway Museum

Aquarium Station, looking towards St George.

A very early view along Front Street, from the area of the Queen Street Station towards, next to the middle-distance trees, Cenotaph Station.

Looking in the opposite direction in later years, with the rolling stock now painted maroon. Note the motor vehicle below the trees at the water's edge.

Shelly Bay	Race Course and Beach	No obvious signs
*#Crawl	Rural Area	Only building foundations remain
*#Bailey's Bay	Caves, Perfume Factory, Golf Courses, Hotels and Sports Park	Tall wall
Coney Island	Rural Area	No obvious signs
Ferry Point	Tourist Attractions: Castle Grotto Caves, Blue Hole Golf Course, and Castle Harbour Speed boats met trains here to carry tourists around the Harbour	No obvious signs
*Oil Docks	West India Oil Co Premises	Dilapidated shelter
Mullett Bay	St George Suburbs	No obvious signs
Wellington	St George Suburbs	No obvious signs
*#St George	Town and Docks	In use by "St George Signs"

Notes:

1.   In addition to the centres and halts listed above and shown on the introductory map (and privilege halts [not shown]), the following halts were built in the period 1935 to 1939:

Cockroach Gulch	
Hunt's Halt	Both east of Sound View Road
Far Rockaway	East of George's Bay Road
Heron's Nest	East of Lighthouse
Yard	Staff use only; east of Hospital
Shelly Beach	East of Shelly Bay
Clay's Halt	East of Crawl
Astor Siding	Also known as Ferry Reach Junction

2.   The stone buildings at Aquarium Station were completed in 1937.

3.   Stations marked * were stone built structures; other passenger shelters, where provided, were of wooden construction.

4.   Stations underlined had passing loops (or were terminii); there was also a passing loop at black Bay Sidings, between Church Road and Lighthouse Stations.

5.   Stations marked # handled freight as well as passengers.

DISTANCES BETWEEN STOPS

(Including (*) stops not shown on introductory map)

Somerset to Hamilton (Cenotaph)

Stop	Distance Between Stops (Yards)	Cumulative Distance (Approx Miles)
Somerset	0	0
Broom Street	600	0.34
Scott's Hill Road	170	0.44
Sound View Road	300	0.61
*Cockroach Gulch	1,200	1.29
*Hunt's Halt	400	1.52
Somerset Bridge	400	1.74
Bridge Hill	470	2.01
White Hill	750	2.44
George's Bay Road	370	2.65
*Far Rockaway	830	3.12
Evan's Bay	750	3.55
Frank's Bay	1,400	4.34
Church Road	930	4.87
Black Bay	800	5.32
Lighthouse	750	5.75
*Heron's Nest	900	6.26
Riddell's Bay	770	6.70
Khyber Pass	1,470	7.53
Belmont Manor	1,000	8.10
Cobb's Hill	800	8.56
Ord Road	1,270	9.28
Elbow Beach	750	9.70
Rural Hill	750	10.13
Hospital	700	10.53
*Yard	1,000	11.10
Middle Road	170	11.19
Cenotaph	800	11.65

Average Speed over Western Section of line, excluding stops: 12.3 mph.

Hamilton (Cenotaph) to St George

Stop	Distance Between Stops (Yards)	Cumulative Distance (Approx Miles)
Cenotaph	0	11.65
Queen Street	570	11.97
Richmond Road	430	12.22
Serpentine Road	230	12.35
Tennis Stadium	600	12.69
Race Course	800	13.14
Pond Hill	670	13.52
Prospect	530	13.82
Devonshire	1,100	14.45
Store Hill	1,530	15.32
Flatts	930	15.85
Aquarium	530	16.15
*Shelly Beach	830	16.62
Shelly Bay	200	16.73
Crawl	1,100	17.36
*Clay's Halt	1,430	18.17
*Bailey's Bay Halt	330	18.36
Bailey's Bay	100	18.41
Coney Island	530	18.72
Ferry Point	1,170	19.38
*Astor Siding	1,170	20.04
Oil Docks	630	20.40
Mullet Bay	970	20.95
Wellington	900	21.47
St George	530	21.77

(Distance this section 10.12 miles)

Average Speed over Eastern Section of line, excluding stops: 11.5 mph.

Average Speed over whole line, excluding stops: 11.66 mph.

(This is not the arithmetic average of the two speeds quoted, as the two sections of the line are of different lengths!)

BRIDGES, TRESTLES, TUNNELS & LEVEL CROSSINGS

The locations of the railway's 33 bridges and trestles are shown on the introductory map. Further details are listed here.

Water Crossings & Foreshore Encroachments

Somerset Bridge - C

Frank's Bay - C

Flatts Bridge - C

Shelly Bay Trestle - T

Five Mile Trestle - C

Burchall Cove Bridge - S

The Crawl Trestle - C

Clay's Bay Trestle - C

Bailey's Bay Trestle - C

Coney Island Bridge - C

Ferry Point Bridge - S

Oil Dock Trestle - C

Burchall Cove Bridge, looking seaward from the small harbour.

Ferry Point Bridge. Note the control cabin and the signal pole for shipping (showing, in this view, the black ball indicating that the channel was obstructed by the swing bridge.

Flatts Bridge, with Aquarium Station just visible on the other side of Flatts Inlet.

Road Crossings & Contouring

Harman's Bay Trestle - T
Parapet Trestle - T
Evan's Pond Trestle - C
Church Road Trestle - C
Mallory Trestle - T
Lighthouse Trestle - T
Riddle's Bay Trestle - C
Sharp's Trestle - T
Warwick Pond Trestle - T
Morgan's Trestle - T
Springfield Trestle - C

Evan's Pond Trestle, viewed from the West. Note, at the observation platform end of the Motor Coach, the refuge provided for any maintenance gang personnel working on the trestle when a train was crossing.

Devonshire Trestle - T

Cox's Trestle - T

Gibbon's Trestle - T

Store Hill Trestle - C

Flatts West Trestle - T

Sisson's Trestle - T

Outerbridge's Trestle - C

Henry's Hill Trestle - S

Gulley Trestle - C

Mullet Bay Trestlen - S

<u>Note</u>: Structures marked 'T' were of timber only construction (except for any concrete plinths or footings); structures marked 'S' were of steel construction; structures marked 'C' were of composite timber, steel and/or concrete.

<u>Tunnels</u>

Rural Hill (between Rural Hill and Hospital Stations, below South Road)

Richmond Road (at the East end of Pitts Bay Road)

A wartime photograph, probably taken in 1942, showing a flat car "squeezing" through the tightly curving Richmond Road Tunnel with construction materials for the United States Navy Base. Notice the "1931 Bermuda Railway" wording above the tunnel mouth. The shrubbery above the stone wall would have been located in Par-La-Ville Gardens.

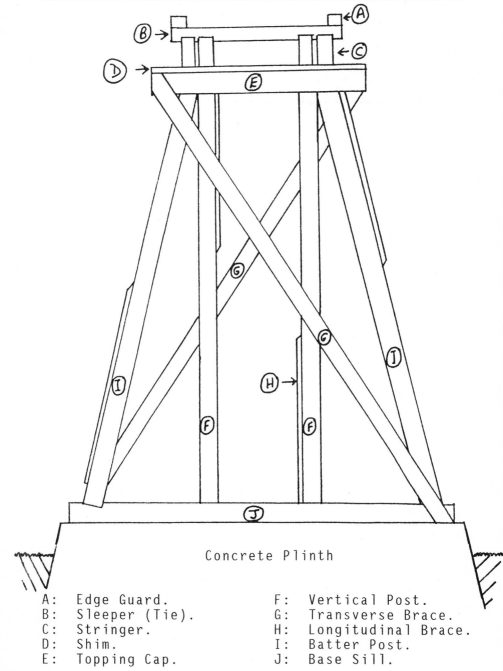

Concrete Plinth

A:	Edge Guard.	F:	Vertical Post.
B:	Sleeper (Tie).	G:	Transverse Brace.
C:	Stringer.	H:	Longitudinal Brace.
D:	Shim.	I:	Batter Post.
E:	Topping Cap.	J:	Base Sill.

Level Crossings (Unmanned)

The road names given below are names in use at the time of the construction of the railway.

St George's Parish:

Main Road (near Wellington)
Ferry Point Road (near Oil Dock West)

Hamilton Parish:

Old Ferry Road
New Road to Bailey's Bay Wharf
New Road at Shelly Bay Race Course

Devonshire Parish:

Toby's Road (Tribe Road No 2)
Frog Lane or Dock Hill Road
Tribe Road No 3

Pembroke Parish:

Serpentine Road
Richmond Road (Church Street extension)
Pitts Bay Road
East Broadway

Paget Parish:

South Shore Road
East Ord Road
Tribe Road No 4A

Warwick Parish:

Cobb's Hill Road   Tribe Road No 3
Tribe Road No 1   Khyber Pass Road
Tribe Road No 2   Tribe Road No 7
Tribe Road No 4
Ord Road (at Belmont Golf Course)

Southampton Parish:

Lighthouse Road   Scott's Hill Road
Tribe Road No 2   Broom Street
Tribe Road No 3   Beacon Hill Road
George's Bay Road   Sound View Road
Main Road (South of Evan's Pond)

Passenger's eye view crossing Somerset Bridge, with
Bridge Hill Station just discernable on the far shore.

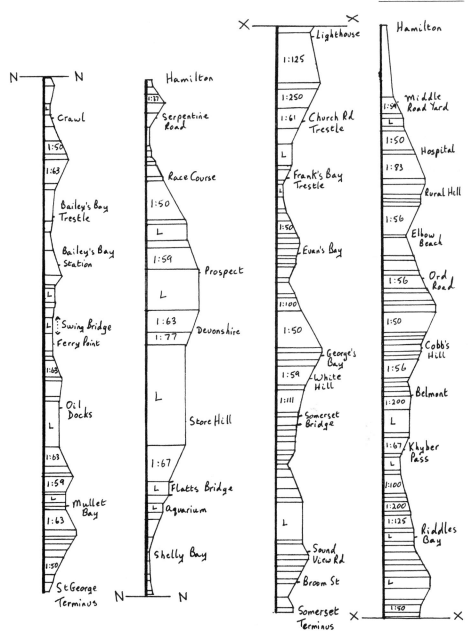

Hamilton to Somerset   Hamilton to St George

GRADIENTS PROFILE

E A S T   B R O A D W A Y   (M I D D L E   R O A D)
L A Y O U T   -   *circa* 1933

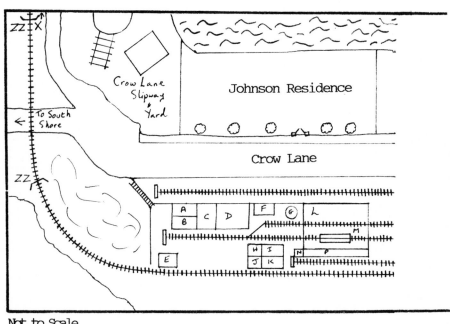

Not to Scale

Key:

A - Chief Engineer's Office
B - Secretary's Office
C - Drawing Office
D - Stores
E - Paint Shop
F - WCs & Showers
G - Cooling Water (for tests)
H/J - Carpenter's Shops
I - Electrical & Brakes Department
K - Foreman's Office & Tool Room

L - Running Shed
M - Maintenance Pit
N - Battery Room
P - Machine Bay
Q - Gasoline Pump
R - HP Wash Water Pump
S - Canteen & Yard Office
T - Key Token Hut
U - Manual Points
V - "Flush" Track

ZZ to ZZ - Springfield Trestle

X -> Line to Somerset

Y -> Line to St George

Based upon a drawing kindly supplied by:
Mr Wm H J Kitchen - October 1992.

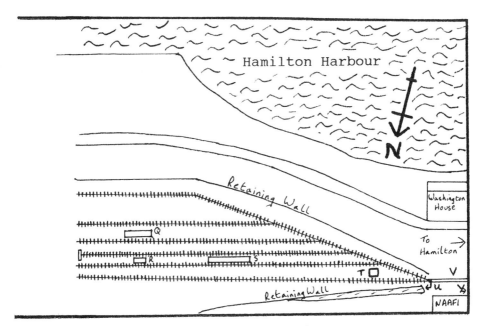

Today. Even the bus station, which replaced the railway yard, has disappeared; the whole site has been built over in the form of a dual carriageway leading into Hamilton from the south and west of the island.

The sheer faces to the north of the yard are still very obvious, and the palm trees still stand alongside Crow Lane - otherwise almost all railway-associated artefacts have now gone.

To those interested in modern history, however, the continuing presence of the old NAAFI building is of interest: it is now a motorcycle sales and repair shop, and its corrugated iron structure is easily spotted by even the most casual of observers!

EAST BROADWAY (MIDDLE ROAD) YARD

A fine detail shot of the yard, looking towards Hamilton from outside the
running shed. A gondola car stands on one of the storage roads, with the
key token hut just visible beyond it - rising behind which can be seen the
through way to Somerset. The larger building in the centre is the canteen
and yard office; the gasoline pump stands below its small "lychgate" cover,
whilst the structure to the right of this houses the HP wash water pump.
Note, off the rails and standing next to the water pump, the "speeder".

A closer view of the "speeder", this time standing at Somerset
Bridge Station and with Harold Kitchen (right) seated thereon.

S T A M P S
A N D   T H E   B E R M U D A   R A I L W A Y

RAILWAY STAMPS

Passengers, and their luggage and bicycles, formed by far the greatest percentage of traffic carried by the Bermuda Railway, but the railway also carried general bulk goods and parcels - the Bermuda Post Office not having a dedicated "parcel post" system. Occasionally, perhaps after the routine postal collections and deliveries had been made, members of the community made use of the railway's parcel traffic organisation to forward letters to other addresses in the islands. Amongst the main users of this service was the West India Oil Co, who regularly sent correspondence to its Headquarters in Pitts Bay Road, Hamilton (near the Richmond Road Tunnel below Par-la-Ville Gardens).

The standard charge for postage of an internal letter in the early years of the railway was 1 penny (1d); the minimum charge for items sent by rail was 3d for up to 6 miles, rising to 6d for distances of 18 miles or more, but existing records indicate that the usual fee charged for letters was 3d no matter how many miles the letter was destined to travel! (For parcels of greater size or weight, prices went up to a maximum of 3 shillings (3/-), or 15p in modern UK money.

The tickets themselves changed in style over the years of the railway's operation, but were all probably produced by the London based Bell Punch Co (see Chapter 2). Overleaf are examples typical of the tickets issued.

"A" This Parcel Stamp was 41 x 78 mm (approx 1½" x 3") in size. printed in red ink on white paper.

"B" A Parcel and Goods stamp of the same size and colour as "A".

"C" Printed in black ink on a range of paper colours, this Parcel Stamp was 32 x 72 mm (approx 1¼ x 2¾) in size. It was perforated, as can be seen, to allow for the lower portion to be used as a receipt.

"A"
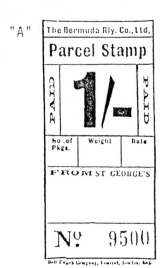

"B"

"C"
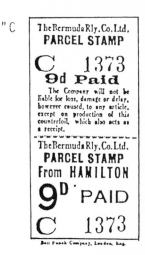

POSTAGE STAMPS

On 22nd January 1987 the Bermuda Post Office issued this set of four postage stamps featuring the Bermuda Railway:

A two-unit train proceeding along Front Street, Hamilton (15 cents).

Train crossing the Springfield Trestle (40 cents).

No 101, at Bailey's Bay Station, en-route to St George with a " pecial" (50 cents).

No 31 pulling away from St George dockside with a boat train from the cruise liner *Prince David* (1 dollar, 50 cents).

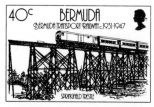

{The stamps proved very popular with residents and visitors alike and today Hamilton's Philatelic Bureau holds no stock of this issue still for sale.}

HAROLD JENNINGS KITCHEN

No book on the Bermuda Railway would be complete without one final reference to Harold Kitchen, who was born in 1885, and spent a lifetime involved in the world of transportation and railways.

A graduate of Derby Grammar School and the winner of the Duke of Devonshire's Science Award in 1901, he was apprenticed to J Stone & Co of Bedford, England, the manufacturers of the universally used "Stone's Patent Train Lighting System".

"The Boss" - Harold Jennings Kitchen (1885 - 1950).

In 1905 he was appointed to the Mechanical Engineers Department to represent the company in its dealings with the Argentine Government Railways, and was promoted to be Assistant to the Chief Mechanical Engineer, Argentine Government Railways, in 1909 - a position that he held until 1914.

On the outbreak of World War I, he returned to England to join TB Balmforth & Co, Iron and Steel Founders, where he assisted in the development of the military tank and was a recognised expert on electric steels, a field in which he made major contributions to manufacturing techniques.

In 1920 he joined the Drewry Car Co as a design engineer and in 1931 was appointed Chief Engineer to the Bermuda Railway Co Ltd. For the whole of the operating period of the railway he was to the fore, putting his technical and managerial skills to full use keeping the railway operating under often difficult conditions, especially under the supply and manpower restrictions in force during the years of World War II. Known affectionately as "The Old Man" by one and all on the railway, he was very much The Boss: always approachable, but so very obviously 100% in charge!

He was very much involved in the survey work that was to lead to the railway's demise and, then, the dismantling of the system - and was the natural choice to be appointed Bermuda's Director of Transportation in 1946 after the metal wheels had ceased to turn. As mentioned in the text, he travelled down to British Guiana to oversee the rebirth of the railway in South America.

Harold Kitchen's heart was never in the task of running the Bermuda bus system; he continued to yearn for the railway years and on 9th December 1950, after a very short illness, he passed away - some would say of a broken heart.

Some indication of the very high esteem in which he was held in Bermuda can be gleaned from praise given when Parliament reconvened after the 1950 Christmas recess. On 8th January 1951, he was glowingly described in the debating chamber as "the man who got the railway running, provided our present transport system and made himself sick through the job." "This colony never had, and never will have, a finer gentleman or a better servant. He had his heart and soul in his work at all times, and used most of his leisure periods working without recompense for the people of this Colony."

Perhaps the best summary of Harold Jenning Kitchen given in Parliament that sad day is simply that by Mr CG Gilbert:

> "He was a railway man, of course.
>
> He didn't particularly go for the buses."

BIBLIOGRAPHY

During my researches I discovered no specialist book dedicated to the Bermuda Railway. My main sources of information were the records of the Bermuda Government Archives Department and the records of the Bermuda Government Works and Engineering Department.

I also made use, in Bermuda, of the facilities of the Public Library, Hamilton, and of the Bermuda Railway Museum, Flatts. In the UK I consulted the records of the Public Records Office, Kew (London), the National Railway Museum, York, and the Royal Commonwealth Society Library, London. In all cases the staff were helpful in the extreme.

Specifically, I offer the following references in the hope that they might be of value to those seeking a deeper knowledge of the system.

The Railway That Vanished: Unpublished manuscript by William Kitchen (1979).

The Royal Gazette: 2nd November and 22nd December 1931, 4th November 1951, 27th July 1958, 30th December 1962, 14th and 15th January 1964.

The Bermudian Magazine: February, July and October 1931 and August 1982.

Bermuda Historical Quarterly: Vol 28, No 2 (1971).

The (British) *Colonial Office Annual Reports (for British Guiana and Bermuda)*: Various dates.

The Government-Owned Railways of British Guiana: report by AJF Dunning, General Manager (1954).

The Railway Gazette: 10th January 1930 and 25th September 1931.

The Railway Magazine: November 1931, April 1986 and April 1987.

British Caribbean Philatelic Journal: June 1992.

Canadian Rail: May 1963.

The American Railroad Passenger Car: John H White Jnr; John Hopkins University Press, Maryland, USA; 1978.

The Bermuda Railway Trail: Bermuda Tourist Board publication.

The publication of this book would not have been possible without the help of those who so kindly gave permission for photographs in their collections to be used - and to whom I extend my grateful thanks.

Photographic Acknowledgements (By Page Number)

The Bermuda Government Archives {* = William Kitchen Collection; # = Bermuda News Bureau Collection; " = Miss K W Burr.}: Frontispiece#, 7", 10*, 11 (Top), 11 (Bottom)#, 12, 14, 19*, 22*, 38#, 79, 82 (Bottom)*, 84, 88*, 89, 96 (Bottom), 100", 101 (Top)*, 103*, 106.

The Bermuda Museum Collection: 6, 21, 25, 48, 49, 81 (Bottom), 91, 95.

C Spanton Ashdown: 18, 26, 29, 31, 32, 33, 83.

Author's Collection: 9.

Balfour Beatty & Co: 13, 81 (Top), 82 (Top), 102.

Ms N Annette Biermann: 52.

Mrs P Cheval: 17, 94.

John Cross: 23.

Mr AA Eastwood: 15.

Mr W Hackney: 20.

David & Anna Hodgson: 34.

William Kitchen: 8, 27, 30, 37, 45, 53, 55, 87, 108, 113.

A Peachey: 96 (Top).

Dora Simpson: 101 (Bottom).

Simon Pomeroy: front & rear covers.

All the modern day photographs, except where listed above, are from the author's collection.

Rail spike found at the site of Sharp's Trestle - 24th August 1992.